পাবলিক অবসিনিটিস

PUBLIC OBSCENITIES

পাবলিক অবসিনিটিস

PUBLIC OBSCENITIES

Shayok Misha Chowdhury

THEATRE COMMUNICATIONS GROUP
NEW YORK
2025

Public Obscenities is published by Theatre Communications Group, Inc., 520 Eighth Avenue, 20th Floor, Suite 2000, New York, NY 10018-4156

TCG books are exclusively distributed to the book trade by Consortium Book Sales and Distribution.

ISBN 978-1-63670-200-1 (paperback)
ISBN 978-1-63670-201-8 (ebook)

A catalog record for this book is available from the Library of Congress.

Book design and composition by Lisa Govan
Cover design by Kameron Neal
Cover photograph by Sailendra Chandra Chakraborty
Author photograph by Beowulf Sheehan

First Edition, June 2025

for Mama
and his dreams

for Mami
and my whole P544 family

for Ma and Baba

and
for Kameron

Pradip Kumar Chakraborty
1945–2023

পাবলিক অবসিনিটিস

PUBLIC OBSCENITIES

Production History

Public Obscenities had its world premiere at Soho Rep. (Sarah Benson, Cynthia Flowers, and Meropi Peponides, Directors) in New York, on February 15, 2023, presented in partnership with the National Asian American Theatre Company (Mia Katigbak, Co-Founder and Actor-Manager; Mona Moriya, Managing Producer). It was directed by the author. The scenic design was by dots, the costume design was by Enver Chakartash, the lighting design was by Barbara Samuels, the sound design was by Tei Blow, the video and projection design were by Johnny Moreno; the dramaturg was Sarah Lunnie, and the stage manager was Alyssa K. Howard. The cast was:

CHOTON	Abrar Haque
RAHEEM	Jakeem Dante Powell
PISHIMONI	Gargi Mukherjee
PISHE	Debashis Roy Chowdhury
SHOU	Tashnuva Anan
THAMMI	Bhadra Chaudhuri
JITESH	Golam Sarwar Harun
BABA	Partha Chowdhury
SEBANTI	NaFis

This production of *Public Obscenities* transferred to Woolly Mammoth Theatre Company (Maria Manuela Goyanes, Artistic Director; Kimberly E. Douglas, Managing Director) in Washington, D.C., on November 14, 2023, and then subsequently to Theatre for a New Audience (Jeffrey Horowitz, Founding Artistic Director; Dorothy Ryan, Managing Director) in New York, on January 17, 2024. There were the following changes: the scenic design was by Peiyi Wong and the stage manager was Tenley Pitonzo.

Characters

CHOTON A Bengali American PhD student, approaching thirty, born in Kolkata, raised in the US. He speaks fluent Bangla and American English.

RAHEEM Choton's boyfriend, Black American, late twenties. A cinematographer.

PISHIMONI Choton's aunt, his father's sister. Born and raised in Kolkata, Bangla is her primary language. Speaking English exhausts her.

PISHE Pishimoni's husband, Choton's uncle, also born and raised in Kolkata.

SHOU Early to mid-twenties, identifies as kothi.*

THAMMI Choton's paternal grandmother, late eighties, bedridden with dementia.

JITESH Caretaker to Thammi and the household help. Doesn't speak English.

BABA Choton's father, appears briefly on FaceTime. His English is Americanized.

SEBANTI A friend of Shou's, an elder. Identifies as hijra.*

*Hijra and kothi are gender categories native to the Subcontinent.

A Note on Language

This is a play in (at least) two languages. The Bangla is deliberately written in Roman script, as phonetically as possible, to make it accessible to Bengalis in the diaspora who may speak the language but not read Bangla script, and also to give English speakers a sense of how the language sounds. Bangla words are undifferentiated from English, typographically. Sometimes the Bangla is translated, sometimes it isn't. The translations point to when there should be English subtitles. In this script, translations are in italicized brackets. The play relies on the specificity of each character's fluency and dialect. Casting should attend to these specificities.

In the script, a slash indicates where the following line begins, overlapping. An em-dash indicates an interruption, either by the next line or by a pivot in the speaker's own train of thought. An ellipsis indicates searching for a thought or a word, or a trailing off.

১। ফিল্ম স্টাডিস

1. FILM STUDIES

A deteriorating house in South Kolkata. Flickering tube lights. Ceiling fans. Cracked plaster. An unsmiling black-and-white photograph of Choton's late grandfather hangs on the wall. Beneath his portrait: an altar, with statues of gods and goddesses, wilting flowers, a conch shell, an offering of sweets. Through an interior window we see Pishe at his computer; the tinny Scott Joplin soundtrack of a virtual pool game tinkles faintly. Choton and Raheem are seated at the dinner table, their backpacks and suitcases plopped in the center of the room. Pishimoni serves them. Choton eats with a fork. Raheem eats with his hands. Pishimoni observes him with delight.

PISHIMONI: Bhaalo chhele, haat diye kheye nay—

(She pinches Raheem's cheek.)

Good boy!
CHOTON: As opposed to me eating with a fork.
RAHEEM: What can I say, I'm a good boy.

PISHIMONI: Uncle has cooked this one. Not very spicy. Little spicy, little oil. Bland aar ki.

RAHEEM: It's delicious—

CHOTON: Aare *bland* na, she doesn't mean bland, she means like—like it's light, it's not / too rich.

PISHIMONI: Hyan light. Simple.

RAHEEM *(Mouth full)*: Tastes like something my mom would make.

PISHIMONI *(Misunderstanding)*: You like it?

CHOTON: Bollo it's something his mom would make.

PISHIMONI: Ki?

CHOTON: Bolchhe or Ma-o erokom ranna kawre.

PISHIMONI: Shedin dekhchhilam TV-te, Vietnam-e naki ora kumro phul diye ekta—

CHOTON: English.

PISHIMONI: I am telling: on TV I saw. In Vietnam they are making—ei kumro'r ingriji ki re?

CHOTON: Mm . . . pumpkin?

PISHIMONI: Pumpkin, yes. In Vietnam I saw they are making the stuffed pumpkin flower. Bengalis we also make this pumpkin flower. We call it kumro / phul.

CHOTON: Or more like squash actually, squash / blossoms.

PISHIMONI: It is not available this time. Next time, you come in October November, I will make it.

RAHEEM: Yes please.

PISHIMONI: But not stuffed, we make it fried. In Vietnam I saw they put prawn, pork. I love to watch this things, in which country which food they are eating.

(She pops a slice of raw onion in her mouth and watches Raheem eat.)

Which food you are eating there in California?

CHOTON: Aabaar ei proshno?

PISHIMONI: Aare I want to know what is the cuisine. Aamaar khub interesting laage. Bibhinno deshe, what type of food is available. Okhaane toh, you have pasta na? Choton, he cook pasta for us.

CHOTON: Awnek Bangali ranna-o korchhi aajkaal. Raheem likes that um . . . oi je Thammi ekta tomato awla rui maachh korto na. I've been making that, but with cod.

PISHIMONI *(To Raheem)*: You like fish?

RAHEEM: I do.

PISHIMONI *(Impressed, to Choton)*: Ba ba Bangali chhele toh puro.

CHOTON: She's saying / you're—

PISHIMONI: Which food you like best, chicken or fish?

RAHEEM: Oh I like both.

CHOTON: Pishimoni, oi deshe toh—ekdin we might have pasta, next day we might have—I don't know, Ethiopian food, Vietnamese / food—

PISHIMONI: Achchha "Rohim" . . . is it a Muslim name?

CHOTON: Jeezus / Chr—

PISHIMONI *(To Raheem)*: Basically you are from which country?

CHOTON: He's American Pishimoni.

PISHIMONI: Parents are from?

(Raheem finishes a mouthful of food.)

RAHEEM: I grew up in Chicago, but my parents are from South Carolina originally—

PISHIMONI: Ei Carolina-tei na Khuki Pishi thhaake?

CHOTON *(To Pishimoni)*: Ota *North* Carolina.

PISHIMONI *(To Raheem)*: My father's cousin-sister, she is also there in Carolina. Very intelligent / lady.

CHOTON: You met her at Rinku's wedding, she was the like, short one with / the—

PISHIMONI: So your mother speaks which language?

CHOTON: Pishimoni—

RAHEEM: She speaks / English.

CHOTON: —or Ma toh o deshe-i bawro hoychhe.

PISHIMONI *(To Raheem)*: Mother tongue is English?

RAHEEM: I mean . . . that's—but yeah, yes—

CHOTON *(To Raheem, conspiratorial)*: I should give her my copy of *Lose Your Mother*.

PISHIMONI: Ki bolchhish?

CHOTON: Kichhu na.

PISHIMONI: Oke Bangla shekha—

CHOTON *(To Raheem)*: She's saying—

PISHIMONI *(Patting Raheem's hand)*: I am telling you should learn Bengali. Bengali is a very sweet. *Beautiful* language.

CHOTON: Hey Raheem knows shushshuri!

PISHIMONI: Shushshuri you know? Shushshuri is very important. *(Extending her arm to Choton)* De toh ektu.

(Choton caresses her arm with his fingertips. Raheem looks slightly crestfallen. Choton notices this. Pishe emerges from the computer room wearing boxers and an undershirt.)

PISHE: Chicken-ta kheyechhish?

CHOTON: Ei je khachchhi.

PISHE *(To Raheem)*: You have tasted?

RAHEEM: Yeah it's delicious, thank you.

PISHE: This one is simple preparation. No oil. Only black pepper, salt—

PISHIMONI *(Offering more)*: Little bit?

RAHEEM: Oh no, I'm good thanks.

PISHIMONI: Good?

RAHEEM: I had way too much already.

PISHIMONI *(To Choton)*: O toh tao khay.

PISHE *(To Pishimoni, outstretching his palm)*: Kothhay ekta mishti dao dekhi?

CHOTON *(To Raheem)*: You OK?

RAHEEM: Mm-hm.

CHOTON: Sure?

(Pishimoni stands with great difficulty and waddles toward the fridge.)

PISHIMONI: Choton you know. He used to take only boiled egg, boiled rice, boiled potato.

CHOTON: This is twenty years ago.

PISHE: So Rohim. How you are finding India?

RAHEEM: Oh it's— I mean so far I've basically only seen this house but it's—

PISHIMONI *(Peering into the fridge)*: Dekhchhina toh . . .

PISHE: Ki?

PISHIMONI: Shawndesh.

CHOTON: We're actually planning on going up to Tikiapara to see where this—

PISHIMONI: Oke Victoria Memorial-e niye ja.

CHOTON: English!

PISHIMONI: You have seen Victoria Memorial?

RAHEEM: I've seen pictures.

PISHIMONI: Beautiful na?

(She kneels heavily in front of the open fridge and peers into its depths.)

CHOTON: Raheem's a big Mrinal Sen fan so we wanted to go see where *Calcutta 71* was / filmed.

PISHE *(Surprised)*: Mrinal Sen?

RAHEEM: Yup. Yeah / my—

PISHE: They know Mrinal Sen in US?

RAHEEM: Mm . . . not really, but—

PISHE: Ray they know, but Sen—

RAHEEM: Yeah, people don't really know him, but *Khandhar* is my dad's like all-time favorite film, so I / basically—

PISHE: Bojho.

CHOTON: Yeah Raheem's dad is a *huge* movie buff.

PISHIMONI: What is his profession? / Your father—

RAHEEM: My dad? I mean he's retired now, but he did all kinds of things, he worked for the postal service for—

CHOTON: Ask him about any foreign film though, who was in it, what year it came out—

PISHIMONI *(To Choton)*: Tui Rohim-ke Dadu'r Rolleicord-ta dekhiyechhish?

(She plops back down in her chair, empty-handed.)

PISHE *(Referring to the mishti)*: Ki holo?

RAHEEM: Did—

PISHIMONI: Bolchhi nei.

RAHEEM: —you say Rolleicord?

PISHIMONI: My father's old Rolleicord is there. You like to see?

RAHEEM: I would love that.

PISHIMONI: Jitesh!

RAHEEM: Oh there's no rush—

CHOTON: Raheem loves old stuff. If it isn't fully disintegrating, he won't even look at it.

RAHEEM: Which is how *you* caught my eye.

PISHIMONI: Ei Jitesh!

JITESH *(Offstage)*: Jaiiiii.

CHOTON: O kintu aamaar-che maatro ek bawchhor'er chhoto.

PISHIMONI: O tor-che chhoto?

CHOTON *(To Raheem, victorious)*: Ha!

RAHEEM: What?

CHOTON: She thinks *you* look older than *me*.

PISHIMONI: Not older. Maane "manly" aar ki.

CHOTON: Ki??

RAHEEM *(Loving this)*: She just call me "manly"?

CHOTON: Ki bolchho?

PISHE: So Rohim, photography is your subject?

CHOTON: Photography na, film, film.

PISHE: Tui je bolechhili photography.

CHOTON: *Director* of photography.

RAHEEM: I mean photography's my subject, that's a true / statement.

CHOTON: Maane cinematography aar ki—

PISHIMONI: Many cinemas are there also very nearby. Old cinema hall. Priya cinema is there, Bijoli, Menoka.

RAHEEM *(To Choton)*: Oh yeah, you holdin' out on me?

CHOTON *(Mouth full of food)*: They're all in Hindi, no subtitles.

PISHIMONI: Oke INOX-e niye ja, English filims are there—

RAHEEM: Oh I want the Hindi films.

CHOTON: I don't.

RAHEEM: 'Cause you're racist?

PISHIMONI: Hindi is there, Bengali is there. English is also there—

(Jitesh enters.)

(To Jitesh) Ei shon, Baba'r camera-ta ektu niye ay toh.

JITESH: Camera?

THAMMI *(Offstage)*: Jitesh?

PISHIMONI: Oi dyakh. Jitesh ghawre dhukle-i thik ter pay.

(Pishimoni opens the door a crack and talks to Thammi through it.)

Ki Ma? Ki holo?

THAMMI: Ke okhaane?

PISHIMONI: Choton eshechhe toh.

CHOTON *(To Raheem)*: My grandmother.

THAMMI: Jawl dao na ektu.

PISHIMONI *(To Jitesh)*: Ei ektu jawl de toh / Ma ke.

PISHE *(To Raheem)*: Sen is not so artistic I think. Tai na? Not like Ray.

RAHEEM: Mm . . . I—

PISHE: Tasteful I mean.

CHOTON: "Tasteful" maane?

PISHE: Dyakh Pather Panchali, Aparajito it is . . . maane this is *art* actually. Isn't it? Even camerawork is . . . ki bolbo? . . . like a painting.

RAHEEM: Huh. That's—

CHOTON: Pishe—

RAHEEM: No that's interesting, I don't know . . . I guess I kind of feel like Sen's films are more . . . painterly than—

PISHE: Sen?

RAHEEM: I mean don't get me wrong, Ray is a genius obviously, I just . . . When I watch his stuff, I feel like . . . like he wants us to forget there's a camera, right?

PISHIMONI *(To Choton)*: O Bangla cinema shawmmonde eto / shikhlo ki kore?

PISHE: See for Ray this is reality toh. He is showing the reality of the life in Bengal.

RAHEEM: *Totally*, that kind of like . . . slice of life, super naturalistic—

CHOTON: Sen was a realist too though.

RAHEEM: Sure . . .

CHOTON: I mean he was definitely pushing against the like melodrama of Bollywood cinema, right? The song-and-dance sequences, the bad lip-synching, the like, longing glances and like, dramatic eye makeup—

PISHE: See, Bengali cinema is not like Hindi cinema / actually.

CHOTON: Ei je—

PISHE: Bengalis we are interested in culture, politics, / this kind of—

CHOTON: This is exactly what I was talking about, Bangalis see themselves as the arbiters of "serious" art. Ei je bolle "tasteful," "bhawdro" . . . these were "*bhawdro*lok" . . .

RAHEEM: What's that?

CHOTON: Bhawdro's like . . . mm . . .

PISHE: Gentle.

CHOTON: Mm . . . not / exactly.

PISHE: This is "gentleman." Bhawdrolok.

CHOTON: . . . gent*eel* maybe.

RAHEEM: But don't you feel like there *is* something kinda campy about Sen's / stuff?

PISHIMONI: Achchha aamaake ektu bawl toh, ki project niye eschhish.

CHOTON: Eita toh ekta . . . documentary thik na, kintu orokom-i project / bolte paaro—

PISHIMONI: Tor na English chhilo subject?

CHOTON: Hyan maane . . . English toh . . . at the PhD level, English maane . . . shudhu literature toh na. Anthropology, performance studies, film studies shawb kichhu miliye . . . maane interdisciplinary ja-ke bawle. Kintu aami toh aashole English thheke gender and women's studies department-e transfer kore giyechhi kaaron—

PISHIMONI: *Women's* studies?

CHOTON: Hyan aamaar advisor jini . . . uni toh Black and Third-World Feminisms niye kaaj kawren, duto department-ei joint appointment. Aar jehetu aamaar research is really looking at . . . India-te . . . specifically Kolkata-tei . . . ki dhawron'er indigenous vocabulary roychhe around gender, sex . . . maane ei concept-gulo ki bhaabe nirmito hoy in a postcolonial / context—

PISHIMONI *(To Pishe)*: Ba ba—

CHOTON *(Uncertain)*: Ki holo?
PISHIMONI: —"ki bhaabe *nirmito* hoy"—

(Pishe smiles.)

CHOTON: Doesn't "nirmito" mean—
PISHE: Tui PhD kore kawtota pekechhish dekhchhi—
CHOTON: Aare shawrol kawthha-i bebohar korlam toh.

(This cracks Pishe and Pishimoni up.)

PISHIMONI: Ma go Ma. Aabaar "shawrol kawthha" . . .

(She tries to get a hold of her giggles. Choton is deflated.)

Aare rege jaash na. Tui kawto shawb bawro bawro kaaj / korchhish.

CHOTON: I haven't even finished my PhD yet Pishimoni.

PISHIMONI *(To Raheem)*: You know my father, he also was English professor.

CHOTON: Anyways long story short, it's kind of a queer archiving project, and there's this dissertation fellowship I'm applying for at U Chicago, so I roped Raheem into coming and filming some interviews with—

PISHE: Achchha Chicago is near to Minnesota, tai na?

CHOTON: What?

PISHE: Na I am having one friend there in Minnesota. O bollo okhaane naki sub-zero zone. Is it so?

CHOTON: I mean . . . it is definitely very / cold.

PISHE: *Whole* year sub-zero?

RAHEEM: It gets pretty hot in the summer. But not like—I mean what y'all have goin' on here is next level.

PISHE *(Enjoying this)*: Next level na? Your Pishimoni, she says to me, why can you not put pant-shirt like a civilized fellow, but I am saying, it is a question of climate. Each one should make adjustment, tai na?

(Pishe indicates his garb. Jitesh enters with the Rolleicord camera, in a leather case.)

PISHIMONI: Eiii je. Dekhi.

PISHE *(To Jitesh)*: Dyakh toh, freeze-e shawndesh'er baaksho-ta paash kina.

PISHIMONI *(Offering Raheem the camera)*: You like to see?

RAHEEM: Oh hold on, lemme just wash my—

(He stands.)

CHOTON *(Pointing to the sink)*: There.

(Raheem walks over to it, bumping into Jitesh.)

RAHEEM *(To Jitesh)*: Oop. Sorry.

(Jitesh squeezes past him and heads to the fridge.)

PISHIMONI: My father you know. Always this camera was around his neck. He called it his another "poite."

PISHE: Ki?

PISHIMONI: Baba bolten na? Ei dyakh aamaar onnyo poite-ta porlam. *(Calling over to Raheem)* You know what is poite?

RAHEEM *(Trying to pronounce it)*: Poy-tay?

PISHIMONI: Poite it is sacred thread. Worn by Bramhon.

CHOTON *(Uncomfortable with the direction this is going)*: O . . . kay.

(Raheem returns to the table.)

RAHEEM *(Referring to the camera)*: Can I?

(Pishimoni hands Raheem the camera. He takes it, reverently.)

PISHE: Ei je Rohim. This is "poite."

(He pulls his poite out of the collar of his shirt and shows it to Raheem.)

PISHIMONI: All Brahmin men they wear it. Boys they receive it twelve thirteen years. Choton still has not received / actually—

CHOTON: And will not be receiving.

PISHIMONI: Keno re? Eta toh aamaader ekta auspicious occasion.

CHOTON: 'Cause I'm not tryna be initiated into the cult of Brahminical patriarchy.

PISHIMONI *(To Raheem)*: Bramhon, you know, this is priest actually.

CHOTON: That's just . . . a totally inaccurate—

PISHIMONI: Aare now it is learned class. Tai toh? You know here we have one Scottish Church College. My father, he was first Indian principal of that college. My brother, Choton's father, he is also professor. But my grandfather see . . . he was walking village to village, performing pujas, marriage, this things. Very poor actually.

CHOTON *(To Raheem)*: This is the origin story.

PISHIMONI: But *my* father . . . he *studied*, by candlelight, in village electricity was not there, then it was British India. Then it was not higher secondary, Eastern India Examination bodh hoy bolto tawkhon. In that examination, my father received top marks. Kintu khub-i gorib chhilen toh. He could not afford to come to Kolkata for studies. That time he was in East Bengal.

(Jitesh deposits the box of sweets on the table.)

PISHE *(To Jitesh)*: Kothhay peli?

JITESH *(Pointing to the fridge)*: Oi je.

PISHIMONI: But that time one Reverend Macaulay was principal of Scottish Church College. He came to know. Village boy. Erokom. Had received top marks. So he offered my father *full* accommodation to complete his studies.

RAHEEM: That's amazing.

CHOTON: But for the record, all of this is *because* Dadu had caste privilege. Right?

(Pishe pops a sweet into his mouth whole.)

(To Pishe) Ei, tomaar na mishti khaowar kawthha na.

PISHIMONI: Bole dyakh toh / ekbaar—
PISHE: Aare bhai what is life without a little sweetness—
CHOTON: Pishe, you have diabetes, this isn't just—
PISHIMONI: Doctor has said, no sweet, no cigarette—
PISHE: Eta toh proshaad.
CHOTON *(To Raheem)*: Proshaad is like, sweets we give as an offering to—

(Pishimoni points to the portrait of Dadu hanging on the wall.)

PISHIMONI: My father preferred this shawndesh.

(Pishe offers Raheem the sweets.)

PISHE *(Mouth full)*: This is Bengali speciality. Nolen gur'er shawndesh.
RAHEEM: Nice, I'll try one in a bit, thanks.
CHOTON: Pishe you have to stop smoking. I'm serious.
PISHE: I am also serious.

(Raheem turns the camera over, examining it.)

PISHIMONI *(Referring to the camera)*: You are interested in this?
RAHEEM: I'm just tryna see what kind of film it takes—
CHOTON: Can you even get film for a camera like this still?
PISHE: Aare photo shop is there. Lake Market-e oi Bombay Photo aachhe na?
RAHEEM: Do you know how old it is?
PISHIMONI: Mm . . . Baba must have purchased Rolleicord . . . I think '62 '63 must have been? That time we used to take summer holiday. Whole family, Ma, Baba, myself, Dadamoni. Choton's father, I call him Dadamoni. So many shots are there. Two of us, on the train compartment to Mussoorie, trekking in Dehradun—
PISHE: He preferred action shot. None of this giving pose, style maara. But zero photos are there of Baba himself actually.
PISHIMONI: Ki bolchho?
PISHE: Aare—
PISHIMONI *(To Raheem)*: My father is there in that photo.

(She points again to the portrait of Dadu.)

PISHE: Bolchhi with this camera, Baba refused anyone else to take photo.

PISHIMONI: What do you know? Baba'r shawmmonde?

PISHE: Eta bhaalo dile.

PISHIMONI: Shaara din computer-e shudhu pitir-pitir. *(To Raheem)* All day he is on the computer, six, seven hours. Playing billiard, sudoku.

PISHE *(To Raheem)*: You have played billiard? Come tomorrow I will show you.

CHOTON: Pishe I'm on a deadline, so we actually have a *lot* of work / to do while—

PISHIMONI: Seven, eight hours he is sitting there—

PISHE: Tumi ki kawro shaara din shuni.

PISHIMONI: Aami toh kichhu-i korina.

(Raheem manages to take the camera out of its leather case.)

PISHE: Ki kawro?

PISHIMONI: Bollam toh. Kichhu-i na. Chuuuup hoye boshe thhaaki. Ekdom lokkhi meye.

(She actively performs silence.)

PISHE: Good. Some peace and quiet.

RAHEEM *(Understanding the camera mechanism)*: Oh wait.

PISHIMONI: Rannabanna, ghawrdor porishkaar, egulo shawb nije-i hoy tai na? Magic.

(The film magazine snaps open. Raheem looks inside.)

RAHEEM: There's a roll of film in here.

(Pishe looks.)

CHOTON: What?

PISHE: Aarebbas . . .
PISHIMONI: Ki?
PISHE: Camera'r bhetor ki roychhe dyakho.
CHOTON: That's . . .
PISHIMONI: Ki? Bujhte paarchhina.

(Pishe takes the film.)

PISHE: This is ancient, you know?
PISHIMONI: Dekhi?
PISHE: Ki kawthha-ta bawle? Fossil fossil. Rohim has discovered—
PISHIMONI: Baba'r tola chhobi?

(Pishimoni takes the roll of film in her hand.)

PISHE: Jitesh?
PISHIMONI: She ki go?

(Jitesh emerges from the kitchen.)

PISHE: Ei dyakh. Awdbhut jinish dekhbi ekta.

(Pishe points to the roll of film.)

Janish ki eta?

(Jitesh stares at it.)

JITESH: Ki?
RAHEEM: We should put it in something, get it out of the light.
CHOTON: There's no way we could still get it developed, right?
RAHEEM: How old is it?
CHOTON: At least . . . what, thirty years?
RAHEEM: I mean especially in this heat, film definitely / deteriorates but—
JITESH: Filim?
PISHE *(Affirmative)*: Hm.
RAHEEM: —it's worth giving it a try.

JITESH: Kothhay chhilo?
RAHEEM: Do you have a Ziploc bag?
PISHIMONI: Ki bag?
CHOTON: Does it need to be Ziploc or—
RAHEEM: Just something that has a good seal.
CHOTON: Like . . . *(Picks up the container of sweets on the table)* . . . something like this?
RAHEEM: Yeah this'll work.
CHOTON: Jitesh Da ekta khaali tiffin'er kouto dibi?
JITESH *(Affirmative)*: Hm.

(He exits into the kitchen.)

PISHIMONI: Bolchho tawkhon thheke-i pore roychhe? Tahle toh Choton'er mukhebhaat'er-i chhobi hawbe.
CHOTON: You think?
PISHIMONI: Tawkhon toh Baba shudhu tor-i chhobi tule beraten shaarakkhon.

(Jitesh returns with a tiffin box.)

RAHEEM *(Taking it from him)*: Thank you.
CHOTON *(To Raheem)*: She's saying it's probably pictures of me Dadu took at my rice-feeding ceremony. 'Cause he died the day right after—
PISHIMONI: Two days after.
CHOTON: Oh tai? I thought it was the day after.

(Raheem seals the film in the tiffin box.)

RAHEEM: Cool if I keep this in the fridge somewhere?
PISHIMONI: Freeze?
RAHEEM: Until we get it developed. It's the best place—
PISHIMONI: Ei Jitesh—
RAHEEM *(Getting up)*: It's cool, I got it.
PISHIMONI: —Kouto-ta freeze-e rekhe ay toh. *(To Raheem)* He will keep it in the freeze.

RAHEEM: Oh. OK. Thank you.

(Raheem hands Jitesh the tiffin box, awkwardly, and sits back down.)

JITESH: Freeze?

PISHIMONI *(Amused)*: Bhaab? Thaanday raakha uchit naki.

(Jitesh looks bewildered. He heads toward the fridge with the tiffin box.)

PISHE *(Calling after him)*: Kheye phelish na kintu!

(This cracks Choton up. Raheem looks confused.)

CHOTON *(Trying to explain the joke)*: He just said like . . . like, "don't eat it."

RAHEEM: What?

CHOTON: Nothing. Never mind, it's— *(Still chuckling)* it's nothing.

২। রিসার্চ

2. RESEARCH

Later that night in the same room, two divans have been pushed together to make a bed. Choton and Raheem are sprawled out, staring at Choton's phone, a bundled mosquito net near their feet.

CHOTON: —or how 'bout just, "Couple from LA, researcher and cinematographer"?

(Raheem gives him a look.)

Come on, no one knows what a "DP" is here.

RAHEEM: I feel like the pic should just be you.

CHOTON: Why?

RAHEEM: 'Cause. It's your project.

CHOTON: Yeah but they're gonna meet both of us if they end up participating.

(Choton rises, phone in hand.)

Plus. You're just hotter.

(He puts his phone down on top of the altar.)

RAHEEM: So you're using me as bait.
CHOTON: Exactly.
RAHEEM: That's fucked up.
CHOTON: Grab these two—

(Choton hands Raheem two corners of the mosquito net. He finds the other two corners and holds them up, demonstrating.)

Lift it up.

(Raheem does so.)

Yeah but keep the net on the mattress, we're basically creating this little mosquito-free zone in there . . .

(They lift up the corners of the mosquito net. Choton inspects it for holes.)

Wow these mawsharis are truly prehistoric.
RAHEEM: What's it called?
CHOTON: Mawshari.
RAHEEM: Maw-sha-dee?
CHOTON: Mawsha*ree.*

(Choton, corners in hand, looks around the room.)

RAHEEM *(Referring to the corners)*: What am I doing with these?

(Choton hangs one corner on a hook in the wall.)

CHOTON *(Pointing)*: How 'bout that hinge?

(Raheem looks at what Choton is pointing to.)

RAHEEM: This?

CHOTON: Yeah tie it around the . . . yeah around the hinge.

(Raheem tries.)

RAHEEM: Like this?

(An ear-splitting snore. Raheem startles.)

CHOTON: Yeah . . . Jitesh Da has a pretty epic snore . . .
RAHEEM: Oh I'm just—

(Raheem peeks through the curtain into Thammi's room.)

CHOTON: I have earplugs.
RAHEEM: He just . . . sleeps on the floor like that?
CHOTON: I mean normally he sleeps in here, but when we're here, he sleeps in Thammi's room.

(Raheem watches Jitesh through the curtain, then returns to tying the net.)

RAHEEM: I don't think I'm doing this right.
CHOTON: Just pull the—here.

(Choton walks over and adjusts the knot.)

And then just make sure to tuck in all the sides. Or actually—get in first and then tuck. Like this, get in super fast so they don't get in . . . and then tuck.

(Choton is inside the net now.)

RAHEEM: How come I haven't seen any mosquitos?
CHOTON: Oh they're here. They're small. The small ones are the bad ones.

(Raheem grabs his phone charger.)

RAHEEM: I need that adapter thingy right?
CHOTON: Yeah in my backpack.

(Raheem unzips. He pulls out a bulky volt converter.)

RAHEEM: This?
CHOTON: No that's the converter for my shaver, there should just be a bunch of 'em in a little pouch. Can you plug in mine too?
RAHEEM *(Referring to the adapters)*: I don't see them.
CHOTON: Bring it over.

(Raheem picks up Choton's heavy backpack and plops it by the bed. Choton reads something in Raheem's face.)

What?
RAHEEM *(Mimicking him)*: What?
CHOTON: I'm just minimizing getting in and out.

(He peers through the netting.)

(Pointing) There. Little pouch.

(Raheem removes two small adapters from the pouch.)

There really is malaria here, I'm not like making it up.
RAHEEM: Where's your charger?
CHOTON: Is it not—oh wait I—

(He produces the charger from his pocket.)

I took it out to charge but then—

(He untucks the mosquito net just enough to hand the charger to Raheem and retracts his hand all in one lightning-swift gesture.)

RAHEEM: Where's your phone?
CHOTON: It's right there on top of the—

(Raheem grabs it.)

(Pointing) Plug it in over there, there's two plug points.

(Raheem walks over to the outlets.)

You can unplug the "Goodknight."

RAHEEM: This?

(He unplugs a vaporizer from the outlet.)

CHOTON: Careful, yeah, there's liquid in there.

RAHEEM: What is it?

CHOTON: It's a—like another anti-mosquito thing.

(Raheem plugs his phone into his charger, the charger into the adapter, and then attempts to plug the adapter into the outlet, but it sticks.)

Wiggle it a little, it'll . . . yeah.

(Raheem looks at his phone.)

RAHEEM: It's not charging.

CHOTON: Did you turn on the switch?

RAHEEM: What switch?

CHOTON: You gotta turn on the switch next to the—

(Raheem flips the switch right next to the outlet.)

RAHEEM: Why?

CHOTON: Can you turn the fan down too? That little knob. Or actually, just turn it off, it's the top left switch.

RAHEEM: Won't it be too hot?

(Raheem tries the top left switch, plunging the room into darkness.)

CHOTON: Oop. Try the top right?

(Raheem switches the tube light back on. It flickers, one end lit. He flips the bottom left switch, and the fan slows and then stops.)

Yeah no you're right, turn it back on. But turn the knob all the way down.

(Raheem obliges. He grabs Choton's phone and plugs it in. Jitesh snores.)

RAHEEM: Should I turn off the lights?
CHOTON: Hold on, now I have to—

(Choton untucks the mosquito net.)

Why do we have to pee? How is that not a thing we've solved yet?
RAHEEM: You pee more than normal people.
CHOTON: 'Cause I drank like four whole Bisleri bottles of water.

(Choton scoots out from the net, re-tucks, and scampers into the bathroom.)

If you drank enough water, you'd have to pee too.
RAHEEM: I know, that's why I don't.

(Raheem takes off his T-shirt and pants. He considers the mosquito net. He untucks quickly and ducks under it. Choton flushes. He scampers back to find Raheem in bed, in his underwear, sitting up very straight, under the net.)

(Referring to the net) I don't know if I like this.
CHOTON: Tuck!
RAHEEM: I did tuck.

(Choton makes a point of tucking Raheem's side of the net further under the mattress. He considers Raheem, newly cloistered.)

CHOTON: You look like a—
RAHEEM: Careful.

(Choton puts up his hands in a gesture of innocence.)

Like a what?
CHOTON: Never mind.
RAHEEM *(Curious now)*: Like a what?
CHOTON: Lights off?
RAHEEM: What were you gonna say?

(Choton flicks off the switch. Darkness. Light filters in through the window between the sitting room and hallway to the bathroom.)

CHOTON: We leave the bathroom light on, Jitesh Da has to take Thammi like ten times a night and each time is a whole ordeal.
RAHEEM: I feel bad.
CHOTON: What?
RAHEEM: That he has to sleep on the floor.
CHOTON: I know . . . it used to fuck with me too, but that's just . . . how he sleeps.

(Choton's cell phone lights up in the darkness.)

Oop.

(He looks at it.)

We got our first message. From . . . "Dreaming Exclamation Point." *(Reading)* "Hot DP." What's DP?
RAHEEM: Um. *(Indicating himself)* Duh.
CHOTON *(Googling)*: What . . . is . . . DP? D . . . P . . . is "double penetration"? What?

RAHEEM: What are you looking at?

CHOTON: Maybe 'cause there's two of us in the pic? *(More googling)* *Oh* . . . "display picture"? Huh. OK. Display picture.

RAHEEM: Look at you learning the local Grindr / lingo.

CHOTON: I know, right? Research!

RAHEEM: It's happening.

CHOTON *(Typing into his phone)*: "Thanks . . . you too . . ."

RAHEEM: Are you lying?

CHOTON: What?

RAHEEM: Do you actually think they're hot, or are you just saying that to get an interview?

CHOTON: No they're cute!

RAHEEM *(Beckoning)*: Me see.

(Choton brings the phone back to bed, with the requisite mosquito-net dance. He hands Raheem the phone.)

Oh OK—

CHOTON: See?

(Choton takes his phone back.)

RAHEEM: So you think an Indian boy is cute?

(The sound of an incoming Grindr message.)

CHOTON: Look we're hoppin'. See? I told you. You're a hot commodity here in Cal.

RAHEEM: What do you mean *I'm* a hot commodity, it's the two of us.

CHOTON *(Reading, with difficulty)*: "Ganja . . . khor." Weed something.

RAHEEM: Ganja?

CHOTON: . . . "Ganjakhor" . . . What is "khor"?

RAHEEM: You call it ganja?

CHOTON: Excuse you, ganja is Sanskrit.

RAHEEM: Really?

CHOTON: Probably "pothead." "Ganjakhor."

RAHEEM: . . . I mean . . . I wouldn't mind some weed . . .

CHOTON: You want to message him? Be forewarned, the weed here is a little . . .

RAHEEM: What?

CHOTON *(Typing)*: "Hi . . . there . . ."

RAHEEM: Or maybe don't use your professional Grindr / for drugs.

CHOTON *(Amused)*: My "professional Grindr."

RAHEEM: I mean . . . that's what it is, isn't it?

(Choton types.)

CHOTON: How 'bout: "We are a couple from the States working on a research project and we're looking to have some conversations with folks who use Grindr in Kolkata." *(Typing)* "Would . . . you . . . be interested?"
Send?

RAHEEM: Do iiit.

(Raheem closes his eyes.)

CHOTON: You sleepy?

RAHEEM: Kinda. You?

CHOTON: Not even a little. It's what, like one P.M. in LA?

(The sound of Jitesh snoring.)

Maybe I need to cum.

RAHEEM *(Sleepily)*: You should cum.

(Choton closes his eyes. He tries to relax.)

CHOTON: I don't not think Indians are attractive, it's just . . . like doesn't it feel like incestuous or something? Like I just know too much. It's like looking at myself in a mirror. Or like . . . looking at my dad. You know? Like I know there will be ear hairs—

(His phone buzzes. For what feels like a long time, too long maybe, Choton messages on Grindr. The modulation of Jitesh's snoring. Raheem dozes.)

(Reading, to himself, tickled) "Purushaali gawndho"?

(Raheem opens his eyes.)

RAHEEM: Hm?

CHOTON *(Looking up from his phone)*: Hm?

RAHEEM: You say something?

CHOTON *(Having a field day)*: Oh I'm just like— This guy's profile just says, "Wishlist," and he's like: one, "Buke ghawno lom," so like, thick chest hair; two, "Bawgol'er lom ebong taar shaathe purushaali gawndho," so like, armpit hair, and then I just love this: "*Purushaali* gawndho," so like . . . I guess like . . . manly musk. And then three, this one's my favorite: "Dui shawkto peshi'r maajhe shaashon kawra'r ek dawndo," which is *just* kind of like . . . genius actually, 'cause like . . . "shaashon kawra'r dawndo" is like a . . . like a rod to like . . . discipline or like . . . yeah like a punishing rod. Between two . . . strong . . . what is "peshi"?

(Choton googles. Raheem observes him, deep in thought.)

RAHEEM: Do you like . . .

(He trails off. After a moment, Choton looks up.)

CHOTON: What?

RAHEEM: Oh nothing I was just . . .

(Choton goes back to typing.)

—like do you like . . . wish I spoke Bangla?

(Choton looks up.)

CHOTON: What? You do speak Bangla.

RAHEEM: Like actually though—

CHOTON *(Teasing)*: You know "begun" and "khichuri"—

RAHEEM: I guess I'm just . . . like we just got here and already I'm like . . . you have this whole . . . like this whole other world . . .

CHOTON: I mean . . . yeah. Yeah this is like . . . I mean this is home, you know?

(Choton's phone dings. Incoming Grindr message.)

Dreaming Exclamation Point wants to meet up.

(Choton types.)

Cool if I tell them to come over at noon?

RAHEEM: Come over here?

CHOTON: Yeah I think it makes most sense to have them come over here, especially at first, so it's a like . . . I don't know . . . a safe space to chat—

RAHEEM: So they want to do an interview?

CHOTON: I mean . . . I kinda wanna hang out a little before springing the question, right?

RAHEEM: So what do they think they're coming over for?

CHOTON: Not a booty call.

RAHEEM: I'm just making sure.

CHOTON: I mean I told them we're here working on a research / project—

RAHEEM: So you *do* want to do an interview—

CHOTON: I mean the application's due Thursday so if they're down yeah, ideally / we—

RAHEEM: So I should set up before they come then.

CHOTON: But see that's what I don't want. I don't want them to see a camera and get all weird, I don't know how out they are, I don't want them to feel pressured.

RAHEEM: OK . . .

CHOTON: I think . . . let's just set up if and when we ask. Right?

RAHEEM: . . . sure. I'm just saying it's gonna take a minute. To set up lights and stuff.

CHOTON: Do we need all that though? I feel like we should keep it pretty natural.

RAHEEM: I mean if you want it to look natural you're gonna want consistent light.

(Incoming Grindr message. Choton looks down. He types. Raheem yawns.)

We should probably set an alarm.

(Choton gives him a look.)

Hey, it's your work, I'm just the cameraman.

(Choton reluctantly complies. Screen light glows on his face.)

CHOTON: What time?
RAHEEM: Is that photo store walking distance?
CHOTON: What photo store?
RAHEEM: I was kind of hoping we could go drop off the film—
CHOTON: In the morning?
RAHEEM: I mean . . .
CHOTON: Yeah I think it's pretty close . . .

(Raheem yawns.)

RAHEEM: Cooli.

(Choton continues Grindr-ing. Just the sound of the clock ticking and Jitesh snoring. Then, suddenly, violently, Choton smacks the side of his head.)

CHOTON: Shit.
RAHEEM: What?
CHOTON: Fuck.
RAHEEM: Mosquito?
CHOTON: Fuuuck.

(Choton looks at his hand. He illuminates his palm with his phone screen.)

RAHEEM: You want your earplugs?
CHOTON: Yeah but then I won't hear it . . .

(He uses his phone screen light to look for the mosquito inside the net.)

These mawsharis are so fucking old.

(He doesn't see the mosquito.)

I guess we can just . . . cover up?

(He pulls a thin bedsheet up around himself. Swaddled, he looks up at the ceiling. He takes a slow, deep breath in and out. He tries closing his eyes. He regulates his breathing. In and out. In and out. A little snore from Raheem. Choton opens his eyes. He stares at the ceiling. He pulls out his phone. It glows on his face. He scrolls on Grindr. He types. He scrolls. He glances at Raheem. Then, making as little noise as possible, he puts his hand down his pants. He touches himself looking at photos on Grindr. He notices the portrait of his grandfather. He considers it. Then, quietly, he gets out of the mawshari, goes over to the portrait of his grandfather hanging on the wall and flips it around, so that his face is hidden. Raheem awakes with a start.)

RAHEEM: What?
CHOTON: Nothing nothing—
RAHEEM: What happened?
CHOTON: Nothing, don't worry. I'm just—

(He gets back into bed.)

—don't worry about it, go back to sleep.
RAHEEM *(Amused)*: Did you / just—
CHOTON: I just . . . felt like he was like . . . watching me. You know?
RAHEEM: Mm-hm.
CHOTON *(Bashful)*: What? Doesn't he look kind of scary?

RAHEEM *(Teasing)*: I don't know, you turned him around—

CHOTON: It's the same one at my parents' place, you've seen it, it's in like every room of the house.

I guess I *always* kind of felt like he was watching me . . .

My dad actually used to— Have I told you this?

RAHEEM: What?

CHOTON: When I first started masturbating? My dad—I think he noticed how much time I was spending in the bathroom, so one night he was just like, you've been spending a lot of time in the bathroom, what have you been doing, and I was so embarrassed I just like, started crying, like, I've been doing this thing, and it feels like I have to pee, and then this white stuff comes out of my nunu, and he was like, it's OK, it happens, and I was like . . . is it bad? And he was like: well, you know . . . it takes up time. And you should think about how you want to spend your time because you only have so much time, and then he pointed to Dadu's picture and was like, you know when Dadu was your age, *he* spent his time studying, by candlelight, in the village, you know same story Pishimoni was telling—

. . .

You know that's the *only* picture I've ever seen of him?

. . .

Chhobi hoye giyechhe . . .

RAHEEM: What's that?

CHOTON: That's what we say when somebody dies. Chhobi is picture.

RAHEEM: Shobi?

CHOTON: It's the aspirated "chh" sound. Like "ch" then "huh"—

RAHEEM: Ch-hobi.

CHOTON: Yeah, chhobi hoye giyechhe. Has become a picture.

I mean that's literally what he is now, right? Just like . . . that *one* picture . . . that after he died, somebody picked to get enlarged and framed and now . . . that's the picture. You know?

That like, Pishimoni puts sweets in front of every—

RAHEEM: What's the word for the sweets again?

CHOTON: Mishti?

RAHEEM: But wasn't there like a—

CHOTON: Oh you mean proshaad? Yeah proshaad is like, any food you put out for like—like it's like milk and cookies for Santa, like *did* Santa eat those cookies? *We* ate those / cookies.

RAHEEM: *Got* it.

CHOTON: But instead of Santa it's a grumpy picture of my grandfather. I mean he and Pishimoni actually had kind of a contentious relationship 'cause she . . . had a love marriage . . . with a younger man . . . couldn't keep a steady job. And my Dadu . . . like the fact that this like guy who got his engineering degree is just like . . . sitting at the computer chain-smoking and playing virtual pool all day, which, by the way, don't feel like you have to humor him with that, every time I come, he asks me, and it's just . . . you know, like the fact that he would walk around the house with just his boxers on drove my grandfather crazy, 'cause my grandfather would like wake up at five A.M., go for a morning walk, take a shower, put on a starched shirt . . . I mean, this is what my dad tells me—

(Incoming Grindr message. Choton looks.)

Look this guy sent a bunch of pics.

(He shows Raheem his phone.)

RAHEEM: Nice.

(Raheem looks.)

He's kinda hot actually.

CHOTON: Yeah?

RAHEEM: Yeah, he has a nice dick.

(Raheem scrolls through the dick pics.)

CHOTON: I thought you were sleepy.

RAHEEM: Yeah . . .

(Choton notices Raheem's erection. He puts his hand on it.)

CHOTON: Oh hello.
RAHEEM: Yeah . . .
CHOTON: We should send him a pic.
RAHEEM: Like take one?
CHOTON: Lemme see.

(Choton reaches for his phone.)

RAHEEM: There's no light though.

(Choton frames a bird's-eye view of Raheem's dick.)

Do it from below. Like put the phone—

(Choton has already positioned the phone between Raheem's legs.)

My face isn't in it right?

(Choton adjusts his angle.)

CHOTON: Hold your dick up? Like up straight—

(Raheem holds his dick up straight.)

Yeah it's covering your face now.

(He takes the pic, with a flash, alarmingly bright in the dark room.)

RAHEEM: Wow.
CHOTON: Sorry—
RAHEEM: I'm blind.
CHOTON: Sorry sorry—

(Choton looks at the picture.)

It looks OK actually.

RAHEEM: Lemme see?

(Choton shows Raheem the picture.)

My balls look huge. Here, lemme take it.

CHOTON: Why don't we just send this one?

RAHEEM: We should both be in it.

CHOTON: He doesn't want to see my dick.

RAHEEM: He literally said "your cocks" plural.

CHOTON: Yeah but . . . is this a cock?

RAHEEM: What are you talking about?

CHOTON: I'm just saying like taxonomically, does it even make sense to categorize my genitalia and your genitalia as the same thing, like . . .

(He indicates Raheem's penis.)

. . . if that's a penis then . . .

(He pulls his boxers down to show his own penis.)

I mean what is this? It's a polyp.

RAHEEM: OK.

CHOTON: It's a little nunu.

RAHEEM: Well I like your little nunu . . .

(Raheem examines Choton's penis. He pulls back his foreskin just a bit. Choton winces.)

CHOTON: Ow. Careful.

RAHEEM: What?

CHOTON: No it's—it's just sensitive.

RAHEEM *(Over it)*: OK . . .

THAMMI *(Offstage)*: Maaaa—

(Choton and Raheem startle at the sound.)

JITESH *(Offstage)*: Ei je. Hyan—
THAMMI *(Offstage)*: Maaaa!
JITESH *(Offstage)*: Ei je. Uthun. O Ma.
THAMMI *(Offstage)*: Hm?
JITESH *(Offstage)*: Eiii je—
THAMMI *(Offstage)*: Ke?
RAHEEM: Is she OK?
JITESH *(Offstage)*: Uthun.

(Sounds of movement from Thammi's room.)

CHOTON: She has nightmares.
JITESH *(Offstage)*: Aaaste, aaste.

(We hear Thammi's voice: incomprehensible, viscous with sleep.)

Haat-ta dhorun. Ekhaane dhorun. Byas—

(The bed creaks: Thammi struggling to rise, supported by Jitesh. Choton and Raheem listen to the muted sounds of their conversation. Backlit, the curtained window is a screen. Thammi, supported by Jitesh: a single, spectral silhouette moving slowly across it. Raheem closes his eyes.)

CHOTON: You OK?
RAHEEM: Mm-hm.

(Quiet. Sounds from the bathroom.)

Did you set the alarm?
CHOTON: Yeah, I set it for 9:30.

(Raheem turns onto his side, away from Choton. Choton, supine, stares up at the ceiling fan. Then he picks up his phone. The sound of Grindr messages. Crossfade to the computer room:

Pishe, lit by the glow of his computer. He is chatting with minnesota76 while playing virtual pool. Pishe is K_gang. Their conversation appears as projected text. The sound of a virtual pool ball hitting a virtual pool ball.)

minnesota76 nooooooo

K_gang OHO BAD LUCK

minnesota76 how do I always do that? :(
minnesota76 that 8 ball has it out for me I swear

K_gang NEXT TIME

minnesota76 u always say that and then u always win :)

K_gang :)
K_gang WHAT TIME IT IS THERE NOW ?

minnesota76 Its 5
minnesota76 in the afternoon

K_gang HERE IT IS THREE THIRTY

minnesota76 am??
minnesota76 go to sleep!

K_gang MY NEPHEW HAS COME ACTUALLY
K_gang FROM USA

minnesota76 Oh nice!

K_gang HIS FRIEND ALSO

minnesota76 That must be nice

K_gang FROM LOS ANGLES

minnesota76	fancy :)
minnesota76	I spent a summer in LA
minnesota76	in high school
minnesota76	my mother thought it would be a good idea to send me to my sister
minnesota76	We never got along
minnesota76	she was four years older
minnesota76	always the princess if u know what I mean
minnesota76	my mother thought it would be good for us
K_gang	UR SISTER LIVES IN LOS ANGELES?
minnesota76	Oh she died
minnesota76	soon after
minnesota76	in an accident
minnesota76	car accident
minnesota76	flew right out the window
K_gang	HEARTIEST CONDOLENCE . . .
minnesota76	it was a long time ago
minnesota76	back then you know . . . seatbelts and such . . .
minnesota76	people were less careful
K_gang	HERE THERE IS LAW
K_gang	POLICE THEY WILL STOP IF YOU DON'T PUT
minnesota76	yeah same here, front and back seat
K_gang	BACK SEAT ALSO ?
minnesota76	they love their laws in St. Paul
K_gang	IS IT IN MINNESOTA ?
minnesota76	St. Paul?
minnesota76	It's the capital
minnesota76	my daughter calls it St. Paul-itics ;)

K_gang	YOU HAVE DAUGHTER ALSO ?
K_gang	I THOUGHT YOU ARE UNMARRIED ?
minnesota76	I am
minnesota76	I mean I was
minnesota76	married
minnesota76	not anymore
minnesota76	One more game?
K_gang	YES !

৩। ভিউফাইন্ডার

3. VIEWFINDER

Raheem sits at the table with the Rolleicord and a new roll of film. He removes the lens cap. It slips out of his hand and clatters onto the table. He claps his hand over it. He examines the camera's lenses.

Jitesh enters with three empty Bisleri water bottles. Raheem looks up and smiles. Jitesh half smiles. He places the bottles on the floor under the Aquaguard water filter, affixed to the wall.

Raheem unclips the camera from its case and gingerly removes it.

Jitesh places one empty bottle on the floor under the Aquaguard. He presses a button. A stream of water pours down, right into the mouth of the bottle.

Raheem snaps open the camera's magazine. He takes the new roll of film and unspools the very end of it. He snaps the spool into the camera. He pulls out the end of the spool and feeds it into a slot at the bottom. Jitesh watches. One bottle of water is full. He swaps it out for another without stopping the stream of water. Not a drop spills onto the floor.

Raheem winds the film until it is taut. He snaps the magazine shut and locks it. Jitesh watches. Raheem looks at the back of the camera. He looks for a viewfinder. He doesn't see one.

RAHEEM *(To himself)*: Huh.

(He turns the camera over in his hands. He notices Jitesh looking at him. Jitesh looks away. Raheem considers every surface of the camera. He stares into the camera lens.)

(To himself) Where the heck . . .

(Jitesh watches, biting his lip. Raheem is staring into the camera lens.)

JITESH: Dekhun—

(Raheem looks up. Jitesh taps the top of the filled water bottle he is holding.)

RAHEEM *(Confused)*: Sorry?
JITESH: Opor-ta khulun.

(He holds out the water bottle and taps the top of it again.)

RAHEEM: Oh . . . I'm good thanks.

(He puts up his hands to refuse the misconstrued offer. Jitesh approaches him. He reaches over and gently pulls open the top of the camera, revealing the viewfinder.)

Oh shit.

(Raheem peers into the viewfinder.)

Wowza.

(Jitesh watches him. Raheem peers through the camera, focusing the image on the bottle of water under the Aquaguard, which has just overflowed and is spilling onto the floor.)

Oops. Your—

JITESH: Hyan?

(Raheem points. Jitesh looks.)

Ei, ei—

(He hurriedly scoots the overfull bottle out from under the stream and replaces it. He hurries into the kitchen and grabs a rag. He lifts the filling bottle an inch and mops up the spilled water around it.)

CHOTON *(From offstage)*: Jitesh Da?
JITESH: Jai!

(The third bottle fills to the top, and he caps it. He picks up the three filled bottles from the floor and hurries into the stairwell. Raheem hangs the camera around his neck, gets up, still looking down into the viewfinder.)

RAHEEM: What a . . . crazy . . .

(Pishimoni enters from the bedroom. As Raheem turns, looking down, he sees Pishimoni in the frame of the viewfinder and startles.)

Jesus—
PISHIMONI: Aarebbas.
RAHEEM: You scared me.
PISHIMONI: Taking photo?
RAHEEM: I'm just getting used to looking through this viewfinder.
PISHIMONI: My father also like this. Always around his neck.
RAHEEM: It's like watching a tiny movie.

(He ambles around the room, peering through the viewfinder.)

PISHIMONI: You have eaten?
RAHEEM: Thanks, yeah, we had some breakfast.

PISHIMONI: Breakfast what you like to have? Omelet toast?
RAHEEM: Jitesh made us some um . . . was it loo-chee?
PISHIMONI: Luchi you like?
RAHEEM: Super tasty, yeah.

(Pishimoni notices the portrait of Dadu flipped around.)

PISHIMONI: E ki?
Jitesh!
JITESH: Jai!
PISHIMONI: Ki aashchorjo.

(Pishimoni walks over to the altar above which Dadu's portrait hangs. Jitesh enters.)

Baba'r chhobi-ta erokom keno bawl toh?
JITESH: Ki?

(She gestures to the portrait.)

PISHIMONI: Baba'r chhobi-ta erom oltano keno? Thik kore de.

(Pishimoni grabs a plate of sweets that is sitting in front of Dadu's portrait. Jitesh reaches on tiptoe to turn the portrait around. Raheem steps in.)

RAHEEM: Here I got it.
PISHIMONI: Or haat toh emni-i pounchhe jaabe.
RAHEEM: What's that?
PISHIMONI: I am saying you are tall. You can reach it just like that.

(Raheem reaches up and turns the portrait of Dadu back around. Pishimoni walks over to the window with the plate of sweets. Jitesh goes to exit.)

RAHEEM *(To Jitesh, indicating the viewfinder)*: Hey. Thank you.

(Jitesh nods subtly in Raheem's direction. Then he exits into the stairwell. Pishimoni sits at the window with the plate of sweets. Raheem watches her through the viewfinder.)

Is that um—is it . . . proshaad?

(Pishimoni looks up, surprised, delighted at the Bangla word.)

PISHIMONI: Proshaad *yes*, aare! You are learning Bengali.

RAHEEM: I'm doin' my best.

PISHIMONI: Every day, I give some sweets to my father, and I do some prayer there. Small prayer. Then afterward, those sweets? We call it proshaad.

RAHEEM: Yeah Choton was explaining it to me—

PISHIMONI: Gods have eaten, now it is proshaad. Now I give some proshaad for the crows.

RAHEEM: Lucky crows.

PISHIMONI: They are lucky *yes*.

(She puts a sweet out on the windowsill.)

You know after my father expired . . . two, three days after . . . I was there in his garden. You have seen it? Upstairs garden?

RAHEEM: I haven't yet.

PISHIMONI: You must see it. For my father, garden it was . . . ki bolbo? Now Jitesh, he maintains. But when my father took care maane . . . it was the most *beautiful* garden.

(She smiles, remembering.)

After he died, I was there on the chhaat, and I saw . . . one crow was there sitting in the chrysanthemum. So I said, hyat! Just like this I said, shoo! Go! But that crow . . . it just . . . like this. Looking at me only. So I approached, waving like this . . . but coming close I saw, the crow's eyes looked *just* how my father's eyes . . . just how he *looked*, you know?

(She puts another sweet out on the windowsill.)

From then on, every day I give some sweets.

(Raheem is watching her intently through the viewfinder.)

RAHEEM: Look at me?

(Pishimoni looks up. Raheem snaps a photograph. Blackout. The photo of Pishimoni develops slowly in an upstage frosted window.)

৪। রুম টোন

4. ROOM TONE

Shou, in low heels and a faux-hawk, perches on the divan, a camera pointed in their direction. Choton sits near them on a rickety stool. Raheem is setting up a softbox light.

SHOU: Aapnaake dekhe kintu NRI mone hoy na. Haab-bhaab puro-puri-i Bangali.
[You don't seem like an NRI you know. Your vibe is totally Bangali.]

CHOTON: Aare Bangali-i toh—
[I mean I am Bangali—]

SHOU: Kolkata'r chhelemeyera-i Bangla bolte paarena aajkaal, edike aapni, baire thheke-o—
[Kids in Kolkata can't even speak Bangla these days, but "aapni," you live abroad and you—]

CHOTON: Achchha aamaake dekhe ki khub bawyoshko mone hoy?
[Do I really seem that old to you?]

SHOU: Hyan? Mote-o na.
[What? Not at all.]

CHOTON: Tahle please "tumi" bawlo, "aapni"-ta / shunte—
[Then call me "tumi" please, "aapni" sounds so—]

SHOU: Aashole Grindr-e dekhe bhaablam nishchoyi kono model'er chhobi laagiyechhe—
[Honestly on Grindr I thought, that has to be some picture of a model he stole—]

CHOTON: Dhyat.
[Oh please.]

(Raheem points a light in Shou's direction.)

SHOU: Aamaar-o kintu boyfriend chhilo ekjon Nigerian.
[You know I also had a Nigerian boyfriend.]

CHOTON *(Surprised)*: Tai?
[Oh yeah?]

SHOU: Mohammedan Sporting'er striker chhilo, aar ki muscle re baba, oof!
[He was a striker for Mohammedan Sporting. And his muscles, oof!]

CHOTON: Aalaap holo ki kore?
[How'd you meet?]

SHOU: Ruby'r odike jeo—Grindr-e *besh* koyekta footballer paabe.
[Go over by Ruby Hospital, there's a bunch of footballers on Grindr out that way.]

CHOTON *(To Raheem)*: Faaascinating.

RAHEEM: What?

CHOTON: The gay Black footballers of Calcutta.

SHOU: O kintu puro straight chhilo.
[He was totally straight though.]

CHOTON *(Amused)*: *Chhilo* hoyto.
*[*Was *maybe.]*

SHOU: Maane?
[Meaning?]

CHOTON: Bollena boyfriend tomaar?
[Didn't you say he was your boyfriend?]

SHOU: Gay'er boyfriend toh straight-i howa uchit.
[Gays' boyfriends are supposed to be straight.]

CHOTON: Oh *I* see.

SHOU: Kothi'r shaathhe toh purushmaanush-i shoy, na ki?

[Who sleeps with "kothis"? Real men right?]

CHOTON *(To Raheem)*: They're saying kothis—

SHOU: Kothi is gay.

CHOTON: Mm . . . not / exactly—

SHOU: Tahle what is gay?

CHOTON: Kothi's more—

SHOU: Receiver. Who receives.

RAHEEM: So I'm the "kothi."

CHOTON: I mean there *is* that valence to it—

SHOU: Hyan? *You* are kothi? No . . .

CHOTON: —but it's also about gender—

RAHEEM *("Guilty as charged")*: I'm the receiver.

SHOU: You are *receiver*?

CHOTON *(To Raheem)*: Shou was saying they met a Nigerian soccer player on Grindr.

RAHEEM *(Amused)*: Oh yeah?

SHOU: I find African men hot actually.

CHOTON *(To Raheem)*: You almost ready?

RAHEEM: Workin' on it.

(Shou makes a pouty face.)

SHOU: Dhyat. Aage'r thheke jaanle ektu sheje aashtam.

[If I'd known, I would have gussied up a little.]

CHOTON: Kothhay? Shundor laagchhe toh.

[What? You look great!]

SHOU: Kaajol-faajol kissu chhaara.

[I didn't even wear any kaajol.]

(Raheem adjusts the camera.)

O Bangla bojhe?

[Does he understand Bangla?]

CHOTON: They're asking if you speak—

(He catches himself.)

(To Shou) Ei sorry, tomaar pronouns jigesh korini.
[Hey sorry, I never asked you your pronouns.]

SHOU: Hyan?
[What?]

CHOTON: Which, I know is actually . . .
jehetu Banglay kono gendered pronoun / nei—
[. . . since there are no gendered pronouns in Bangla—]

SHOU: Maane?
[Meaning?]

CHOTON: Maane ingriji-te jemon "he, she," "his, her" . . . Banglay toh sherokom kichhu nei—
[Like in English how we have "he, she," "his, her" . . . in Bangla we don't have anything like that—]
—right, we just have . . . what, registers of formality like . . . "uni, onaar," "ini, enaar," "enaara / enaader—"

SHOU: "Ma, maati, / maanush."
["Man, mother, motherland."]

CHOTON: —but the idea of *gendered* pronouns is actually kind of an Anglocentric imposition—

SHOU: Ek cup chaa paowa jaabe ki?
[Could I get a cup of tea?]

CHOTON: Ei sorry kichhui offer korini! Jitesh Da?
[Sorry, I didn't offer you anything! Jitesh Da?]

JITESH *(Offstage)*: Jaiii.
[Coming!]

CHOTON *(To Raheem)*: You want tea?

RAHEEM: Mm . . . no I'm good, thanks.

(Raheem places a boom mic in front of Shou. Shou winks at Raheem. Raheem smiles.)

SHOU *(Conspiratorial)*: Baari-te aar keo roychhe?
[Is anybody else home?]

CHOTON: Hyan aamaar Pishemoshai, Pishimoni roychhe bhetore—
[Yeah, my uncle and aunt are both inside—]

SHOU: She ki, aamaar okhaane aaste boltam.

[What? You should have come to my place.]

(With a wink) Complete privacy.

(Jitesh enters.)

CHOTON: Ei ektu chaa khaowabi please?

[Hey, could you make us some tea?]

JITESH: Shawbai khaabe?

[For everyone?]

CHOTON: Duto korle-i—

[Just two—]

RAHEEM: Actually . . .

CHOTON: Yeah?

RAHEEM: Yeah, I'll have some.

CHOTON: Tahle teente kawr.

[Three then.]

JITESH: Dudh chini?

[Milk and sugar?]

CHOTON: Aami toh shudhu liquor.

[Just black for me.]

(Referring to Raheem) Aar oke *ektu* khaani chini dish, beshi mishti pawchhondo kawre na.

[And give him just a little sugar, he doesn't like it too sweet.]

SHOU: Shunun aamaar ei shawb kawm mishti-fishti cholbena, full du chaamoch deben. Thik aachhe toh?

[Listen, "not too sweet" isn't going to cut it for me, give me two full spoonfuls, OK?]

(Conspiratorial) Aar Dada, du khaana biscut hawbe ki?

[And brother . . . could I get a couple biscuits too?]

CHOTON: Awboshyoi hawbe.

[Of course.]

(To Jitesh) Biscut'er kouto-ta niye aashish toh.

[Bring the biscuit tin with you.]

JITESH: Thiiik aachhe.

[Sure.]

(Jitesh exits.)

SHOU: Aami puro biscut-ta dubiye khete bhaalobaashi. Chaa-te gole jaate puro—

[I like to dip the whole biscuit in. So it melts in the tea and just—]

CHOTON: Aare aami-o tai kortam!

[That's what I used to do!]

SHOU: Aami *ekhono* kori, kochi bachcha'r moton.

[I still do. Like a little baby.]

CHOTON: They're saying they like dissolving their biscuits in—

SHOU: I make biscut soup actually.

RAHEEM: Oh yeah?

SHOU: Like a baby.

(Shou makes a baby face.)

RAHEEM *(To Choton)*: Do me a favor? Look on the monitor and let me know when the mic's out of frame?

(Choton steps over to the monitor. Raheem holds the mic in frame.)

CHOTON: Yup, it's in frame.

(Raheem lowers the mic very slowly.)

In.
In.
In.
In . . .
OK, out.

SHOU: Achchha o deshe ki eta-i aapnaader kaaj? Maane rojgaar-ta ki ei bhaabe-i kawren?

[So in the US is this your job? Like is this how you make money?]

CHOTON *(Chuckling)*: Rojgaar bishesh korina, aami ekhono PhD niye-i lore jachchhi, aar Raheem toh freelance director of / photography—

[We don't really make money, I'm still slogging through my PhD, and Raheem is a freelance director of photography.]

SHOU *(Impressed)*: Director? Oishaala.

[Director? Wowza.]

CHOTON: Maane lighting, camerawork ei shawb / aar ki.

[Meaning lighting, camerawork, things like that.]

SHOU: *Avengers: Endgame* dekhechho?

[Have you seen Avengers: Endgame*?]*

CHOTON: Hyan?

[What?]

SHOU: Dyakhoni? Phaataphaati cinema. Dekho, INOX-e cholchhe.

[You haven't seen it? It's a killer movie. Go see it, it's playing at INOX.]

CHOTON *(To Raheem)*: Wanna go see *Avengers: Endgame*?

(Raheem glowers at him.)

I thought you wanted an authentic Kolkata cinema experience. There'll be an intermission, all the sexy scenes will be cut—

SHOU: I also want to dance in filims actually.

Kintu okhaane jemon cinema niye-i pawrashona hoy, aamaader ekhaane toh sherokom na. Ekhaane toh dance it is—

[But there how you can just study cinema, it isn't like that here. Here dance—]

Especially hip hop, Bollywood, this things—it is seen . . . maane awposhawngshkriti aar ki.

CHOTON: "Awposhawngshkriti" maane?

[What's "awposhawngshkriti"?]

SHOU: "Awposhawngshkriti" maane . . . maane "perverted culture."

["Awposhawngshkriti" means . . . like "perverted culture."]

CHOTON: *Oh* achchha, bujhechhi . . .

[Oh OK, I get it . . .]

(He writes in his notebook.)

So like a . . . like the culture being perverted by like . . . immoral Western influences / right?

SHOU: Shedin jemon Lake'er dhaare boshe selfie tulchhilam. Hawtath gombhir gawlay ekjon pulish ki shawb bolte laaglo, public jaygay naki awshleel bebohaar nishiddho, erokom awposhawnshkriti'r chote-i naki desh'er ei awbosthha, aare / bhai—

[Like the other day, right? I was taking selfies by the lake. Suddenly this cop with this deep voice starts saying all kinds of stuff like, "Obscene behavior in public is illegal, this kind of perverted culture is ruining our country," I mean—]

CHOTON: Ki dekhe bollo?

[What did he see that—]

SHOU: Ei je. Erokom. Heel awla choti, orna pore chhobi tulchhilam. Taarpawr aamaar bag tene dekhte laaglo. Oi Shurokkha Foundation aachhe na? Maajhe maajhe giye condom tule aani, free-te paowa jay bole. Du chaarte pamphlet-o chhilo, shegulo dekhe Mama bollen naki distribution of pornographic material, aare bhai kaake distribution, shawb toh nijer jonnyei tulechhilam!

[Just this. Like this. I was wearing heels and a scarf and taking pictures. Then he started looking through my bag. You know the Shurokkha Foundation? Sometimes I go get free condoms from there. I had a couple pamphlets too, and Mr. Cop was like, "distribution of pornographic material," like excuse me, distributing to who sir? I got them for myself!]

CHOTON: Kisher pamphlet?

[What kind of pamphlet?]

SHOU: Oi je AIDS awareness pamphlet hoy na?

[You know those AIDS awareness pamphlets?]

CHOTON: And he called them pornographic?

SHOU: Yes! He sayed . . .

. . . oi je ki ekta Section er under-e aachhe na?

[. . . isn't there some like Section or something?]

CHOTON: 292 hyan, distribution of obscene materials.

SHOU: Oi, oi obscene material-i.

[Yes that! That "obscene material."]

CHOTON: Huh! That's crazy. That these like . . . like even these educational pamphlets, there's still like a fear of them being . . . ki bolbo. Arousing?

SHOU: Aare aami toh shei kaarone-i tulechhilam, chhobi-gulo ja hot na. Pulish'er-o pawchhondo hoychhilo mone hoy. Pant'er bhitor baanra-ta spawshto bojha jachchhilo.

[I mean that's why I got them, 'cause the pictures are hot! I think the cop liked them too. I could see the outline of his "baanra" right through his pants.]

CHOTON: Ki kawthha-ta bolle?

[What's the word you just used?]

SHOU: Kon-ta?

[Which?]

CHOTON: Bolle pulish'er ki-ta / dyakha—

[You said you could see the cop's—]

SHOU: Baanra-ta?

[His "baanra"?]

CHOTON *(To Raheem, behind the camera)*: You're getting this right?

RAHEEM: Not yet.

CHOTON: Wait what?

SHOU: Besh bhaalo size'er chhilo kintu—

[It was a nice size too—]

CHOTON: Ei ek second pause korte paari?

[Hey, could we pause for a second?]

I just want to make sure we get this on camera—

RAHEEM *(To Shou)*: Sorry . . . is it Shou?

SHOU *(Mimicking his cadence)*: It is Shou.

RAHEEM: Is it cool if I put a little powder on your nose?

SHOU *(To Choton)*: Baba, ki service.

[Oh wow, what service!]

RAHEEM: There's just a little shine I wanna get rid of.

SHOU: Come come. Hollywood level.

(Raheem daubs the tip of Shou's nose with a makeup sponge.)

RAHEEM: And—sorry. Can you just run your hand through your hair once?

SHOU *(Confirming)*: Hair?

RAHEEM: Yeah there's a flyaway that's catching the light.

SHOU: Like this?

RAHEEM: That's great thanks.

CHOTON: We good?

RAHEEM: Yup. Let's just get thirty seconds of room tone.

CHOTON: Can we do it after?

RAHEEM: . . . sure.

CHOTON: Or fine, let's just do it now. Sorry shuru kawra'r aage we just need thirty seconds of silence to capture the sound of the room.

SHOU: My hair it's OK?

RAHEEM: Looks great.

(To Choton) Wanna take a look at the shot real quick?

(Choton looks.)

CHOTON: Bollam shundor laagchhe.

[Told you you look great.]

SHOU: Dekhi?

[Let me see?]

(Choton turns the monitor to show Shou. Shou fixes their hair, using the monitor as a mirror.)

CHOTON: Thik aachhe?

[Good?]

(Shou takes a flower from a little vase and puts it behind their ear.)

SHOU: Hnu. Ebaar thik.

[Yeah, now it's good.]

(Choton turns the monitor back.)

CHOTON: Start korlam tahle? Thirty seconds silence? Starting . . . now.

(They sit in silence. The silence is anything but silence: car horns and street sounds filter in through the open window. Then, fifteen seconds in, Jitesh's voice perforates. In the kitchen, he is singing as he waits for the tea to steep.)

JITESH *(Singing)*: Ki ba gurguraaya diya daake gawgon hoilo kaala . . .

CHOTON: Are you serious?

(Loudly) Jitesh Da?

(The singing continues.)

RAHEEM: Don't worry / about it.

CHOTON *(Louder)*: O Jitesh Da!

JITESH: Jaii.

RAHEEM: —I think we got / enough.

CHOTON: Well either way we need quiet while / we—

RAHEEM: I mean—

(A dog barks, echoing through the stairwell. Jitesh enters.)

CHOTON: Hyan re, aamra khaanikkhon ekta interview record korchhi, tai / jodi—

[Hey, we're recording an interview in here for a little bit, so if you could—]

JITESH: E Ma . . .

[Oh no . . .]

(Jitesh sticks out his tongue and bites it, in embarrassment.)

CHOTON: Na kono awshubidha nei just ektu—

[No, no problem it's just—]

SHOU: Aapnaar gawla-ta kintu phaataphaati Dada.

[You've got a killer singing voice, brother.]

JITESH: Hyan?

[What?]

SHOU: First class. Ma Kali'r dibbi bolchhi.

[First class. I'm serious.]

CHOTON: Ei just aawaaj-ta jodi *ektu* / kawm—

[If we could keep the noise down—]

JITESH: Hyan hyan, thik aachhe.

[Sure sure, of course.]

CHOTON: Just ektukkhon'er jonnyo.

[Just for a little bit.]

SHOU: Eshe ekta gaan shonaaben kintu.
[And then I want to hear you sing.]

(Jitesh smiles abashedly as he exits.)

Yaarki na!
[I'm not kidding!]

CHOTON *(To Raheem)*: Are we still rolling?

RAHEEM: Yup.

CHOTON: OK, so . . . tumi je bolchhile, Lake-e tomaar ei je ghawtona-ta—
[OK, so you were saying, this thing that happened to you by the lake—]

SHOU: So interview it has started?

CHOTON: I mean don't think of it so much as an interview, just think of it as a conversation—

SHOU: It should be English toh?

CHOTON: Bangla, English, whichever.

SHOU: English is no problem.

CHOTON: Sure sure, I'm just saying feel free to move between . . . Maane aamaaro hoyto mone hawbe, oh, ei jinish-ta Bangla-tei bolte shubidha / tai—
[I might also feel like, oh it's easier to talk about this thing in Bangla, so—]

SHOU: But Bangla how they will understand?

CHOTON: Who?

SHOU: Maane eta toh ekta American filim-i hawbe na ki?
[I mean this will be an American film, right?]

CHOTON: Aare subtitles toh aachhe, don't worry—
[Well there are subtitles, so don't worry—]

SHOU: OK, OK. So some subject is there or . . . ?

CHOTON: Well I'm interested in this question you're bringing up, 'cause it seems to me like, just tomaar presence-ta-i . . . just the way you looked that day was enough to be seen as obscene. Right? The way you were dressed, je / bhaabe—

(Jitesh enters with tea.)

SHOU: Eiii je, chawmotkaar.

[Here we go, perfect.]

(Jitesh places a cup of tea, and a small plate with biscuits and sweets on a low table in front of Shou.)

JITESH: Biscut.

CHOTON *(To Raheem)*: Is that in the shot?

RAHEEM: I think it's fine if it's in there.

SHOU: O baba, duto mishti-o?

[Oh wow, two sweets too?]

JITESH: Bhai'er jonnyo ekhaane raakhlam?

[I'll keep this one for brother here?]

(Jitesh places Raheem's tea and sweets on the table next to him.)

RAHEEM: Oh thank you.

(Jitesh hands Choton his tea.)

CHOTON: Aami kintu ekkhuni mishti khaabona.

[I don't want sweets right now.]

(Jitesh keeps the plate of sweets and goes to exit.)

SHOU: Kothhay chollen Dada? Gaan-ta ja-te miss na hoy.

[Where are you going brother? What happened to my song?]

(Jitesh looks to Choton.)

Oi je polligeeti gaichhilen ekta?

[That folk song you were singing?]

JITESH: . . . aapnaara toh byasto . . .

[. . . you all are busy . . .]

SHOU: Kothhay byasto? Chaa khete khete toh aar shooting hawbe na—

[Busy with what? It's not like we're filming while we have tea—]

CHOTON: Raheem bolchhilo—

[Raheem was saying—]

(To Raheem) We're cool to record with the tea, yeah?

RAHEEM: Whatever y'all want.

SHOU: Chaa-ta kintu Dada hebbi hoychhe.

[The tea is super, brother.]

(Jitesh looks again to Choton.)

CHOTON: Tor ranna hoychhe?

[Have you made lunch yet?]

JITESH: Bhaat chaapiyechhi.

[I just put the rice on.]

SHOU: Aare du line awntoto geye jaan.

[Sing us a couple lines at least.]

(Jitesh stands awkwardly, plate of sweets still in hand.)

JITESH: Jeta gaichhilam?

[The one I was singing?]

SHOU: Hnu, shuni.

[Yeah, let's hear it.]

(Jitesh clears his throat. He hesitates.)

JITESH: Ektu khaani-i gaichhi.

[I'll sing just a little bit.]

(He begins singing. A folk song. It's tentative at first, but as he sings, he gains conviction, and a certain quiet falls over the room. Raheem turns the camera toward him. When the verse is finished, he stops abruptly.)

SHOU *(Thoroughly impressed)*: Oof! Phaataphaati.

[Wow! Amazing.]

(To Raheem) You should shoot *this*, na? Local talent.

(Raheem gives Shou a thumbs-up from behind the camera. Choton shoots him a look.)

JITESH *(Noticing the camera)*: Hei Raam.
[Oh lord.]
SHOU: Bhaari mishti kintu aapnaar gawla.
[Your voice is so sweet.]

(Pishimoni enters.)

PISHIMONI: Baba biraat production cholchhe toh.
[There's a serious production going on!]
CHOTON *(Under his breath)*: Are you serious right now?
PISHIMONI *(Waving to the camera)*: Hello.
SHOU: Nomoshkaar Pishima.
[Greetings Auntie.]
PISHIMONI: Mishti peyechho?
[Did you get the sweets?]
SHOU: Peyechhi, Dada'r gaan-o shunchhi—
[Got the sweets, listening to brother's singing—]
PISHIMONI: Aare jaanabi toh bondhu eschhe toder—
[You should have said your friend was coming—]

(She plops down onto the divan.)

CHOTON: —Pishimoni—
PISHIMONI: —ghugni baaniye raakhtam.
[—I would have made some ghugni.]
CHOTON: —bollam na, aamra ektu ei ghawre—
[—I told you, we're working in here—]
PISHIMONI: Ei ei sorry! Disturb korlam? Mone holo gaan-taan hochchhe.
[Sorry! Am I disturbing? I thought I heard singing, so I thought I'd peek in.]
SHOU: Dada'r gaan'er recording cholchhe, "Sa Re Ga Ma"y paathano hawbe.
[We're recording brother's singing to send to "Sa Re Ga Ma."]

PISHIMONI: Tai naki?

[Really?]

CHOTON: Pishimoni—

PISHIMONI: Ankita ke dekhechho?

[Have you seen Ankita?]

SHOU: Hm.

[Yup.]

PISHIMONI: Awshaadhaaron na? Rawng-ta jodiyo ektu moyla, kintu gawla khaana maane bhaaba jay na.

[Isn't she amazing? She's a little dark, but her voice . . . I mean . . . it's unbelievable.]

SHOU: Puro Lata Mangeshkar—

[She sounds just like Lata Mangeshkar.]

PISHIMONI: Kintu ekbaar bawlo toh aamay, eto shundor ekta meye, erokom blouse keno porte jay bawlo toh?

[But tell me though. Why does such a pretty girl have to wear that kind of a blouse?]

CHOTON: Pishimoni—

PISHIMONI: She don't need actually. Tai na? Beauty is *there.* Pujo-te dekhbi *shawb* erokom haat-kaata blouse pore aajkaal thakur'er shamne selfie tulchhe—

[At Pujo you'll see everyone's taking selfies in front of the goddess, wearing sleeveless blouses—]

SHOU: Thik bolechhen.

[You're absolutely right.]

PISHIMONI *(To Raheem)*: This is not our culture actually. Marwaris they wear this type, OK.

SHOU: Aajkaal toh Bangla shona-i jay na Kolkatay.

[You can't even hear Bangla in Kolkata these days.]

PISHIMONI: Ei dyakho, tomaar naam-ta-i toh jigesh korlam na—

[Hey look, I didn't even ask you your name—]

SHOU: Aamaar naam Shou.

[My name's Shou.]

PISHIMONI: Shou?

SHOU: Shoubhik-ta bawddo purush-purush shonay—

[Shoubhik sounds too manly—]

CHOTON *(To Shou)*: Kintu tumi je bolchhile—

[But weren't you saying—]

PISHIMONI *(To Jitesh)*: Achchha tui haate mishti niye daanriye aachhish keno orokom, statue'r moton? De ekta shawndesh. Khaowa uchit na jodiyo.

[Hey, why are you standing there like a statue holding those sweets? Give me a shawndesh. Though I really shouldn't.]

(Jitesh hands her the plate of sweets. She puts one in her mouth.)

Janish, diabetes naki pa diye dhoke, krimi'r moton?

[Did you know diabetes comes in through the feet, like tapeworms?]

SHOU: Aapnaar ki sugar? Aamaar Ma'r-o sugar niye awnek jhaamela.

[Do you have blood sugar? My mother also has problems with her sugar.]

PISHIMONI: Aar bolish na. Kawto ki je control-e raakhte hoy.

[Don't even get me started. I have to watch everything I eat.]

(Choton whispers something in Raheem's ear.)

RAHEEM *(To Choton)*: —I got it, don't worry—

SHOU *(To Jitesh)*: Dada, oi gaan-ta jaanen ki? Menoka maathhay dilo ghomta?

[Do you know that song, brother? "Menoka hide your head in shame?"]

JITESH *(In the affirmative)*: Hnuu.

[Sure.]

SHOU: Khub favorite gaan aamaar. Sheje nechechhilam-o ekbaar, Pujo'r function-e.

[It's one of my favorite songs. I even dressed up and did a dance at puja once.]

(Shou rises and begins to recall a dance.)

Dekhi Menoka'r roop-ta mone pawre kina.

[Let me see if I can remember the moves.]

PISHIMONI: Aamaar gawlay toh shur-i nei, tai chirokaal Jitesh'er bhawjone-i baari'r pujo-tujo shawb chawle. Baba bolten oishworik gawla.

[I can't even hold a tune, so it's always Jitesh who sings at our family pujas. My father used to say his voice is "heavenly."]

SHOU: Shotti-i tai.

[It really is.]

PISHIMONI *(Pointing)*: Oi je. Aamaar Baba.

[There. That's my father.]

CHOTON *(To Shou)*: Ei naach-ta kawbe korechhile?

[So when did you do this dance?]

SHOU: Oi class eight naagaad. Ma bechaari praay awggyan hoye giyechhilo dekhe, chokhe kaajol, tawktawke laal lipistick, kintu aami bhai shortcut'er moddhye nei. Korle, thik moton-i kawra uchit. Tai na?

[Around class eight? My poor mother almost fainted seeing me wear kaajol and bright red lipstick. But I don't take shortcuts. If I'm going to do it, I should do it for real, right?]

(Choton resumes his interviewer's position, looking at Raheem to make sure he is filming Shou, which he is.)

CHOTON: Aar ei naach-ta ki kono—

[And did this dance have any—]

SHOU: Dhyat. Mudra-ta mone-i aaschhe na. O Dada, gaiben naki ekbaar?

[I can't remember the gestures. Brother, will you sing it once?]

(Singing) ". . . jaamai chirokaalo nyangta lo nyangta, Menoka / maathhay dilo ghomta . . ."

[". . . an always naked son-in-law . . . Menoka hid her head in shame . . ."]

(Jitesh joins in.)

JITESH: "Menoka mathhay de lo ghomta"

["Menoka hide your head in shame."]

SHOU: Aha.

JITESH: "Bechhe bechhe korli jaamai
Bechhe bechhe korli jaamai
Chirokaali nyangta lo nyangta
Menoka maathhay de lo ghomta"
["This is who you picked to marry your daughter? He's always naked! Menoka hide your head in shame."]

(Jitesh's singing is punctuated by Shou's rhythmic footfall and vocal exclamations. Pishimoni sings a line or two with him, off-beat, off-key. Raheem, in his element, follows the action with his camera. Choton watches, impotent, as the interview devolves into a full jam session.)

"Koti'r tawte baagham bawra
Nikawmmata ganjay day dawm
Koti'r tawte baagham bawra
Nikawmmata ganjay day dawm
Aabaar haate tishul maathhay jawta
Haate tishul maathhay jawta
Thik bhikaari'r dhawng-ta
lo dhawng-ta"—
["He just hangs out by the river, wearing his tiger skins, puffing on his ganja. With his trident and his dreadlocked hair, he looks just like a beggar."]

SHOU: O ho!

(Raheem leaves his video camera focused on Jitesh and grabs the Rolleicord. Choton notices. Peeved, he tries to get Raheem's attention.)

JITESH: "Menoka maathhay de lo"—
["Menoka hide your head in shame"—]

(Raheem snaps a shot of Shou. Blackout. The photo develops slowly in the upstage frosted window.)

৫। এক্সপ্রেশান

5. EXPRESSION

Pishe as K_gang, chatting with minnesota76, playing pool, smoking a cigarette. Their conversation appears as projected text.

K_gang	IS IT COLD THERE NOW ?
minnesota76	not too bad
minnesota76	past the worst of it I would say
K_gang	HERE IN CALCUTTA APRIL IT IS VERY HOT
K_gang	TODAY ALMOST 40 DEGREE
K_gang	CENTIGRADE
minnesota76	40 celcius?
minnesota76	I was gonna say 40s not so bad it was 40 something here today
K_gang	40 IS WHAT DEGREE CENTIGRAFE ?
K_gang	CENTIGRADE

minnesota76	lemme look it up
minnesota76	says its 4.444 :)
K_gang	4 DEGREE ?
K_gang	THAT WE NEVER SEE
K_gang	HERE BELOW 20 WE PUT MUFFLER CAP
minnesota76	Whats a muffler cap?
K_gang	MUFFLER IT IS "SCARF"
minnesota76	Aaah got it
minnesota76	here a muffler is something for your car
minnesota76	makes it quiet
K_gang	AGAIN EXCELLENT !
K_gang	THIS IS BANK SHOT
minnesota76	:)
K_gang	U KNOW THIS IT REQUIRES KNOWLEDE OF GEOMETRY
K_gang	TRIGONOMETRY
K_gang	SO YOU ARE MATHEMATCIAN ?
minnesota76	HA!
minnesota76	Definitely NOT
K_gang	THEN HOW YOU ARE ACHIEVING THIS ?
minnesota76	playing with you!
minnesota76	Getting plenty of practice :)
K_gang	MY WIFE
K_gang	SHE SAYS THIS IT IS ADDICTION
K_gang	I AM SAYING HOW IT IS DIFFERENT ?
K_gang	ALL DAY YOU ARE WATCHING TV

K_gang	I AM LIVING IN-LAWS HOUSE
K_gang	THIS IS THE TROUBLE
K_gang	WIFE SHOULD BE LIVING IN HUSBANDS HOME
K_gang	ISNIT IT ?

minnesota76	Isnt that a little "old-fashioned" ;)

K_gang	I COULD NOT EARN
K_gang	THAT ONLY
K_gang	EARNINGS WERE NOT ADEQUATE
K_gang	WE CALL IT ' GHARJAMAI '
K_gang	THAT HUSBAND IS UNSUCCESSFUL

minnesota76	I dont know . . .
minnesota76	I dont think money is everything

K_gang	YOU ARE YOUNG . . .
K_gang	SO WHY YOU ARE CHATTING WITH ' OLD ' MAN :)

minnesota76	I think . . .
minnesota76	a nice man is worth something
minnesota76	Plus . . .
minnesota76	I find you very good looking . . .

(Choton's voice calls from the stairwell.)

CHOTON: Pishe?

minnesota76	Is that OK to say?

(Choton enters the house, an envelope and a set of small, square photos in his hand. Raheem enters behind him, the Rolleicord around his neck.)

CHOTON: O Pishe—
PISHE *(Startled)*: Hm?

CHOTON: Aashbo?
[Can I come in?]
PISHE: Daanra, ek minit.
[Hold on one minute.]

(Pishe puts out his cigarette. Choton walks over to the dining table, looking at the photos.)

Khelbi naki billiard?
[Want to play billiards?]
CHOTON: Edike esho.
[Come over here.]
PISHE: Ki hoychhe?
[What is it?]
CHOTON: Chhobi-gulo eschhe.
[We picked up the photos.]
PISHE: Daanra.
[Hold on.]

(Choton coughs.)

CHOTON: Cigarette khachchho?
[Are you smoking?]
PISHE: Na toh.
[No . . .]
CHOTON: Na maane?
[What do you mean no?]
I can smell it.

(Pishe types.)

K_gang	YOU ALSO ARE LOOKING
K_gang	LOVELY

PISHE: Chawshma-ta niye aaschhi.
[Let me get my glasses.]

(Pishe logs off. He enters the sitting room, glasses in hand.)

CHOTON *(Thrusting the photos toward Pishe)*: Ei dyakho. Eta ki Dadu?
[Look at these. Is this Dadu?]

(Pishe sits at the table. He peers eagerly over the bridge of his glasses at the pile of small, square, black-and-white photographs. He looks closer. His brow furrows.)

Ki?
[What?]
Eta Dadu?
[This is Dadu?]

(Pishe looks at the next photo.)

PISHE: Tullo ke egulo?
[Who took these?]
CHOTON: Wait wait—
Dadu *erokom* dekhte chhilo?
[Dadu looked like this?*]*
Seriously? I thought—
PISHE *(Calling to Pishimoni in the other room)*: Shunchho?
[Are you listening?]
CHOTON: —like . . . what???
He looks so . . .

(Seeing the next photo, Pishe lets out a little laugh, despite himself. Choton peers closer.)

(To Raheem) I mean this is like . . . a photoshoot right?
PISHE *(Calling to Pishimoni in the other room)*: Kothhay gele?
[Where'd you go?]

(Choton looks closer.)

CHOTON: Is that mustache drawn on?

PISHE: Baba toh goph raakhten na.

[Baba didn't keep a mustache.]

CHOTON: It is totally *drawn* on—

PISHIMONI: Ki hoychhe?

[What's going on?]

(Pishimoni appears in the doorway, sleepy-eyed.)

PISHE: Ei dyakho.

[Look.]

(Pishe hands her the photos.)

PISHIMONI *(Eagerly)*: Hoychhe develop? Dekhi.

[Did they develop? Let me see.]

(She sits. She looks at the photos. The others watch her nervously.)

Na bujhte paarchhina.

[No I don't understand.]

CHOTON: Aamra-o bojhar-i cheshta korchhi.

[We're also trying to understand.]

PISHIMONI: Ke eta?

[Who is this?]

(Choton looks to Pishe, worried.)

CHOTON: Pishimoni—

PISHE: Chawshma-ta niye esho.

[Go get your glasses.]

PISHIMONI *(To Choton)*: De toh chawshma-ta. Khaat'er opor roychhe.

[Will you get me my glasses? They're on the bed.]

(Choton exits into the bedroom. Pishimoni squints at the photos. Choton returns with the glasses. Pishimoni puts them on. She looks at the photos, one at a time. Her face is expressionless.)

CHOTON: Pishimoni . . . eta toh Dadu.
[Pishimoni . . . this is Dadu.]

(Pishimoni looks through the photos again silently.)

I thought he hated being photographed.
(To Raheem) I mean is there any way he could have taken them himself?

(Raheem peers at the photos.)

RAHEEM: Mm . . . I mean . . . *maybe* if he had a self-timer but like . . .

(He looks closer at one photo.)

—no 'cause look, see that shadow?

(Choton looks.)

CHOTON: Oh you're right . . .
RAHEEM: Plus you can tell he's looking at someone 'cause he's looking up above the lens . . .

(Everyone considers the photos.)

They're kind of amazing.

(Pishimoni abruptly puts down the photos and walks out of the room.)

CHOTON: Pishimoni—
RAHEEM: Shit / I'm—
CHOTON *(Getting up)*: Pishimoni—
PISHE: Aare chhere de.
[Let it go.]

(Choton follows her.)

RAHEEM: —sorry, I / didn't—

PISHE: What sorry? Nothing to be / sorry.

RAHEEM: I just meant like . . . as photographs they're—shit, I'm so / sorry—

PISHE: One must accept reality. Isn't it? She is not accepting. Thirty plus years father is gone, still she is telling, "My father, my father," aare!

(He points to the photos of Dadu in front of him.)

She is my wife, still what she is thinking that I don't know, what I am thinking, that she don't know. So? This is reality.

(He walks over to the bookcase-cum-altar and retrieves a hidden pack of cigarettes. He looks up at Dadu's portrait.)

You know man cannot be god actually. Isn't it?

(There is a plate with two sweets on the altar. He pops one in his mouth. He offers the second sweet to Raheem.)

Have some.

RAHEEM: No no—

PISHE: Sure?

RAHEEM: Really, I'm good.

(Pishe eats the second sweet. He puts the cigarette in his mouth and goes to light it.)

PISHE *(Referring to the cigarette)*: Is this a problem?

RAHEEM: Not at all.

PISHE: Good. For Choton it is a disturbance.

RAHEEM: Oh I'm aware.

(Pishe tries lighting his lighter.)

PISHE: Constitution it was always little bit weak actually.

(Pishe tries the lighter again. It still doesn't light.)

Dhyat.

RAHEEM: Here, I have mine.

(He pulls his lighter out of his pocket and hands it to Pishe.)

PISHE: Ei excellent.

(Pishe lights his cigarette with Raheem's lighter. He hands the lighter back and offers a cigarette.)

You like to have?

RAHEEM: No I'm good thanks. Thank you though.

(Pishe inhales deeply, his eyes returning to the photographs. He exhales a cloud of smoke.)

PISHE: You know my father-in-law. Always he sayed to me, "Be serious. You are not serious." Now look. Look at this serious fellow.

(He gestures to the photos, tickled, vindicated.)

I knew him since I was twenty-three years. But I *never* saw this . . . ki kawthha-ta bawle? This *expression*. How he is looking here. At the camera.

(He takes another puff of his cigarette.)

What he is *thinking*, that I don't know. But he is thinking *something*. Isn't it? Just with an expression.

RAHEEM: I mean that's what I meant honestly, the photos catch this kind of . . . glint in his / eye—

PISHE: Amazing na?

RAHEEM: —but I wasn't thinking about the fact that this is her *dad*, I was / just—

PISHE: Have you seen *Jalsaghar*?

RAHEEM: Is this . . . like a film or—

PISHE: Yes yes, this is Satyajit Ray, aare what is the— *(He clucks his tongue)* —in English I believe it is called "Concert / Room"—

RAHEEM: Oh! That's um—I think it's *The Music Room* / in—

PISHE: Ki *expression.* Isn't it?

RAHEEM: Oh for sure.

PISHE: Maane with facial expression alone—

RAHEEM: I mean that scene when he looks in the mirror is iconic.

PISHE: Simple expression. Without dialogue.

(Another long drag from his cigarette.)

You know I had one dream this like actually, some years back. Vivid dream. I am in a cinema hall . . . and on the screen, I am seeing one young executive . . . holding a portfolio . . . leather portfolio . . . entering a hotel room. And from that hotel room, through the window, can be seen a swimming pool. OK? And in the swimming pool, he saw a beautiful-looking girl. And this executive, he very much has a want to meet this girl. Then the shot changes. That girl is now sitting inside the room, wearing a green sari. And the girl says to him, I have a story to tell: when I was twelve, thirteen years, I was walking by the river . . . suddenly a strong flood has come, and with my hands in the air like this saying save me, save me . . . Then the picture faded. Then next scene is showing one elderly gentleman, wearing a dhuti. And until now actually shots were in color, OK? This one it became black and white. Elderly gentleman he is going, basket on his head . . . as he is going, absentmindedly like this, as if he is catching a fly and putting in the basket. Catching. Putting. And seeing this I turned to my friend and sayed—all this time there was no friend there, suddenly my friend was next to me—and I sayed to him: this is trash! This cinema has no meaning. And just as I sayed this, my sleep broke. And finding Pishimoni next to me, I sayed to her . . . what a strange and beautiful cinema I have seen. Just like this I sayed. "What a strange and beautiful cinema."

RAHEEM *(Genuinely taken aback)*: Whoa.
PISHE: Just like this.
RAHEEM: That's—
PISHE: Byas. This only.

(Raheem considers something.)

RAHEEM: This might be weird but . . . would you mind telling it to me again?
PISHE: Again?
RAHEEM: So I can record a voice memo? If the details change, that's OK, I'd just—
PISHE: Detail meaning?
RAHEEM: I just mean—
PISHE: Here there is no detail to change, executive he was in white dress.
RAHEEM: Wait, hold on, lemme just—

(He pulls out his phone and opens a voice memo.)

Do you mind?
PISHE: No, no problem.

(Raheem presses record.)

RAHEEM: And actually—can I take a picture of you? Just like you are right now, don't—

(The Rolleicord is still around Raheem's neck. He picks it up, opens the viewfinder. Pishe takes a drag of his cigarette.)

That's great, just like that. Look at me.

(Pishe looks at the camera, smoke curling out of his mouth. Raheem snaps a photo.)

Sorry you were saying . . . the executive—

PISHE: Executive was in white dress. Smart white dress. OK? Portfolio was tan color. Leather portfolio. Now, if he is coming to the hotel first time or he has come before, that I do not know. I am telling only what I am seeing in the cinema.

RAHEEM: And this guy is *in* the film?

PISHE: *In* the film, yes.

RAHEEM: So in the film, you're watching this guy enter this—

PISHE: Hotel room on the second floor. Erokom, like this. He opens the door, window is there, and through the curtain, he sees a woman in the swimming pool. OK? And this girl is beautiful to see. So he has a want to see her. This only. It appeared so. Then when he turns, woman is there . . . wearing a sari . . . bottle-green sari—

RAHEEM: In the hotel room?

PISHE: Inside the room. Sitting on the bed. And just as he turns, she says to him, "You have an interest in me, and I have got a story to tell." And then she says this is what happened to me. That I was walking by the bank of the river. When I was twelve, thirteen years. Suddenly there was . . . rush of water. With my hands up like this, "Save me, save me." This much only.

RAHEEM: And when the woman is telling this story, you're seeing the story in the film?

PISHE: Yes, seeing the story. There are no words mind you.

RAHEEM: After she says, "I have a story to tell you"—

PISHE: No no, she did not tell to the man either, "I have something to say." Only her expression was that. That "I have got a story to tell."

RAHEEM: Oh so the woman didn't say anything.

PISHE: No didn't say. Only in her expression.

RAHEEM: *Got* it.

PISHE: Gentleman, lady, neither says anything. No words are there. OK? He only picturized the thing. The picture came to him . . . that she is walking by the river and then the water came. Byas. After this, black and white. Village man is walking, basket on his head. And he is catching something. With his hand, catching, putting. As if he has become insane.

RAHEEM: Oh I see, so he's not actually catching flies.

PISHE: Actually nothing is there. Just catching, putting.

RAHEEM: I kinda like the image of him catching flies.

PISHE: It could be flies, it could be some . . . ki bawle? He is harvesting something, I don't know. I don't know anything more. Just that only. Then suddenly I sayed to my friend—suddenly my friend is next to me, I sayed to him: "What a terrible cinema." And then I woke up, Pishimoni is there, I sayed to her, "What a wonderful cinema I saw. Wonderful dream."

(A beat.)

You know. This will be a short film. Maximum one minute. No more than that. If it's possible. How it is done that I don't know. That it is your subject.

(Raheem smiles.)

Hyan? You are director.

RAHEEM: Ha!

PISHE: You make it.

RAHEEM: I'm not a director.

PISHE: You are / director.

RAHEEM: Director of photography / means—

PISHE: Yes.

RAHEEM: I mean I support the director, but it's not like I make my *own* films—

PISHE: Why not?

RAHEEM: Like I'm responsible for the camerawork—

PISHE *(Understanding)*: Achchha, I see.

RAHEEM: I mean I'm not saying—I don't know . . . like if everyone's just "having a vision" then . . . I mean somebody has to actually make the thing, right?

PISHE: Because—

RAHEEM: Which isn't to say— *(He laughs)* I feel like I'm doing the thing where I'm making it seem like DPs aren't actual artists, we are, we're / just—

PISHE: Because in my dream . . . there I am seeing what the camera is seeing. Isn't it? Only this. Vision is the camera. Byas.

(Raheem considers this.)

RAHEEM: And it's like a ghost story? Am I getting this right? 'Cause if the woman drowned when she was—

(Choton reenters, on FaceTime with his father, Baba.)

CHOTON: Ei je dyakhachchhi. Daanrao.
[Hold on, let me show you.]

(Seeing him, Raheem stops recording. Choton coughs from the cigarette smoke.)

Aabaar cigarette?
[Again cigarette?]

PISHE: Daanra.
[Hold on.]

CHOTON *(To Raheem)*: My dad's on FaceTime.

(Pishe puts out his cigarette. Choton turns the phone to show Raheem. Raheem waves.)

RAHEEM: Hello.

BABA: Ei, how are you Raheem?

(Baba's English is Americanized.)

RAHEEM: I'm doin' well, how are you all doin'?

BABA: Doin' well, doin' well.

CHOTON *(To Pishe)*: Nijer shorir'er jawtno na korte chaile aamaar kichhu bawla'r nei, kintu bolechhi toh, cigarette'er dhonway aamaar asthma'r awshubidha hoy—
[If you don't want to take care of your own health, I have nothing to say, but I've told you, cigarette smoke exacerbates my asthma—]

BABA: Everything is OK there?

CHOTON: Ei je.
[Here.]

(Choton holds up one of the photographs to the phone.)

PISHE *(To Baba)*: Hello Dadamoni.
BABA: Hmm, ki awbosthha?
[Yeah, what's the situation?]
CHOTON: Dekhte pachchho?
[Can you see it?]
BABA: Dekhi.
[Let me see.]
CHOTON: Daanrao.
[Hold on.]

(Choton tries to center the photo.)

Ghaabre jeo na kintu.
[Don't freak out.]

(He repositions the camera.)

Ebaar dekhte pachchho?
[Can you see them now?]

(There's a momentary pause.)

BABA: Kothhar thheke aashlo egulo?
[Where did these come from?]
CHOTON: They were inside Dadu's camera.
PISHE: Bolechhilam Bombay Photo-tei—
[I told them go to Bombay Photo—]
BABA: So the film was inside the camera?
CHOTON: Yeah, we just picked them up.

(Pishimoni enters and walks purposefully over to her father's altar.)

BABA: Tullo-ta ke?
[Who took them?]

CHOTON: I mean it must have been Thammi, right?

BABA *(Unsure)*: Thammi?

PISHE: Ma-ke kintu konodin camera dhorte dekhini—
[I've never seen Ma use a camera—]

CHOTON: We could ask.

BABA: Aare ekhon ki "ask," ekhon toh mental awbosthha khub-i weak.
[What "ask"? Now her mental state is very weak.]

(Pishimoni notices the sweets are missing.)

PISHIMONI: Jitesh!

JITESH *(Offstage)*: Jaiii—
[Coming!]

BABA: De toh ek second Pishimoni-ke.
[Give me to Pishimoni for a second.]

CHOTON: Daanrao. Pishimoni—
[Hold on. Pishimoni—]

(Jitesh enters.)

PISHIMONI: Proshaad-ta kothhay gelo?
[Where's the proshaad?]

JITESH: Proshaad . . . toh—
[The proshaad . . . was—]

PISHE: Aami kheyechhi.
[I ate it.]

(Pishimoni stares at Pishe.)

PISHIMONI: Ki?
[What?]

(Pishe stares back.)

PISHE: Khaabo na Baba'r proshaad?
[I'm not allowed to pay my respects?]

BABA: Chhobi-gulo aar ekbaar dyakha / toh.

[Show me the photos again?]

JITESH *(To Pishimoni)*: Notun mishti enechhi.

[I bought new sweets.]

PISHIMONI: Aare dhyatteriki!

[Oh come on!]

(Jitesh exits into the kitchen. Pishimoni arranges prayer items on the altar.)

CHOTON *(To Baba)*: I'll take pics of them and text them to / you—

BABA: No no, don't do that—

CHOTON: It's not like he's naked—

BABA: OK, OK—

JITESH *(Reentering)*: Mishti.

[Sweets.]

BABA: —aar kauke dyakhaashna kintu chhobi-gulo.

[—but don't show the pictures to anyone else.]

PISHIMONI: Notun mishti debo kaak-ke? Paagol naki?

[You want me to give fresh sweets to the crows? Are you crazy?]

(Jitesh is unsure what to do.)

De. Ekhaane de.

[Here. Give it here.]

(Jitesh hands the sweets to Pishimoni.)

CHOTON: Daanrao call back korchhi ektu pawre.

[Hold on, I'll call you back in a bit.]

BABA: Achchha OK OK.

(Choton hangs up. He begins taking snaps of the photos of Dadu with his phone. Pishimoni places the sweets in front of Dadu's photo. She clasps her palms together and begins reciting a mantra. Choton looks at Pishe. Pishe gives Choton a tired look.)

PISHE: Ki bolbo bawl?
[What am I supposed to say?]

(Pishimoni fixes him with a stare.)

PISHIMONI: Tomaar bawla'r toh kono jayga-i nei.
[You have no place to say anything.]

PISHE *(To Raheem)*: I was telling, na?

PISHIMONI: Kaar baari-te tumi eta hyan? Shawrgo thheke-o maanush-ta tomaar bhawron-poshon kore jachchhe.
[Whose house are you in, huh? Even from heaven, the man is still paying your bills.]
Baba'r pension chhaara shawngshar cholto ki? Maashe maashe Dadamoni taaka na paathale—
[Without my father's pension, how would we live? If my brother didn't send money every month—]

CHOTON: Pishimoni—

PISHIMONI: Na, he should hear, na?
Konodin nijer paaye daanrate paarlona. Chirodin onnyer khaabar-i kheye gelo—
[Never stood on his own two feet. Always eating someone else's food—]

(Pishe gets up abruptly and walks toward the computer room.)

Hyan jao, bawsho. Shaara jibon shudhu computer-e pitir-pitir—
[Yeah go, sit. Whole life, just tap-tapping away on the computer—]

PISHE: Tumi Baba'r chhobi-ke pujo kore jao, kaak-ke khaowao—
[You just keep praying to your father's picture and feeding the crows.]

PISHIMONI: Baba'r naam mukhe enona. Konodin chenoni Baba-ke.
[Keep my father's name out of your mouth. You never really knew him.]

(Pishe lets out a little laugh.)

PISHE: Aar tumi jyano kawto chinte.
[And you clearly knew him so well.]

(His eyes gesture toward the photos laid out in front of Choton. Then he steps into the computer room. Pishimoni turns to Choton.)

PISHIMONI: De toh chhobi-gulo.
[Give me the pictures.]
CHOTON: Ki holo?
[What happened?]
PISHIMONI *(Hand outstretched)*: De aamaake.
[Give them to me.]
CHOTON: Pishimoni, I'm just trying to—I've never even seen any pictures of Dadu, I just want / to—
PISHIMONI: Then have some respect.
CHOTON: I—
PISHIMONI: OK?
CHOTON: —keo bolchhena je—
[—no one's saying—]
PISHIMONI: This is my father's house. Show him some respect.
PISHE *(Under his breath)*: House?

(Pishe is staring at the computer screen. The sound of virtual pool.)

PISHIMONI: Ki bolle?
[What did you say?]
PISHE *(So she can hear)*: Bollam "house" kothhay? Eta toh ekta mausoleum.
[I said what "house"? This is a mausoleum.]

(Pishimoni stands very still. Then she brings the sweets over to the window. With a cold calm, she places them in a line on the windowsill. Choton, Raheem, and Jitesh watch. The sound of car horns and crows cawing outside.)

৬। হ্যান্ডসাম

6. HYANDSOME

Jitesh walks into Thammi's room. Choton follows, photographs of Dadu in hand. Raheem grabs the Rolleicord and positions himself in the doorway. Only Raheem is visible onstage; the rest we see silhouetted through a curtained window. As the Rolleicord focuses on Thammi, projected in the upstage frosted window, we see what the camera sees: Thammi lying in bed, skeletal, frail. Choton sits on a low stool at her bedside, photos in hand. Jitesh is barely visible at the edges of the frame. We don't see his face, but we hear his voice. The camera refocuses.

JITESH: Ma? Ke eschhe?
[Ma? Who's here?]

THAMMI: Hm?

JITESH: Oi dyakho ke eschhe.
[Look who's here.]

THAMMI: Ke?
[Who?]

JITESH: Naati. Aapnaar naati.
[Grandson. Your grandson.]

CHOTON: Ki go.

JITESH: Bhaalo nei aajke.

[She's not well today.]

CHOTON: Ki go Thammi. Ghumochchhile?

[Were you sleeping Thammi?]

THAMMI: Hm?

CHOTON: Ghumochchhile?

[Were you sleeping?]

(She doesn't respond.)

Dekhi, chawshma koi tomaar?

[Let's see, where are your glasses?]

(Jitesh grabs her glasses from the nightstand and gently puts them on her face. It's clear she doesn't like it.)

Ei dyakho.

[Look at this.]

(Choton shows her one of the photos.)

Dekhte pachchho?

[Can you see?]

(Thammi ignores him and looks directly into the camera.)

Ei chhobi-gulo ki tumi tulechhile?

[Did you take these pictures?]

(She continues staring at the camera.)

O Thammi, ektu edike taakao.

[O Thammi, look over here for a sec.]

(Choton puts the photo in her line of sight. She continues to look past it toward the camera.)

Ke eta?
[Who is this?]
Chinte paarchho?
[Do you recognize him?]
Dadu naki?
[Is it Dadu?]
Eta Partho.
[This is Partho.]

THAMMI: Hm?

CHOTON: Partho. Tomaar bawr.
[Partho. Your husband.]

(She lets out a little snort.)

THAMMI: Aamaar biye-i hoyni.
[I'm not even married yet.]

CHOTON *(Amused)*: Tai naki? Kawto boyosh tomaar?
[Oh is that right? How old are you?]
Tomaar chhelemeye aachhe?
[Do you have children?]
Naam ki tomaar chhelemeye'r?
[What are your children's names?]
(Feeding it to her) Kawmol . . .
[Kawmol . . .]

THAMMI: Kawmol, Ketoki.
[Kawmol, Ketoki.]

CHOTON: Hnu thik. Ketoki phul. Kawmol phul. Thik kina?
[That's right! Ketoki flower. Kawmol flower. Isn't that right?]

THAMMI *(Inaudibly)*: . . . kawmolo mukulo dawlo . . .

CHOTON: Ki bolle?
[What'd you say?]

THAMMI *(A little louder)*: . . . kawmolo mukulo dawlo . . .
[. . . the kawmol flowers blossoming . . .]

CHOTON *(To Jitesh)*: Ki bolchhe?
[What's she saying?]

JITESH: Ki Ma? Pawchhonder gaan naki?
[What do you think Ma? You like that song?]

(Jitesh sings.)

Aaji kawmolo mukulo dawlo khulilo
Aaji kawmolo mukulo dawlo khulilo
Dulilo re dulilo
Manoshoshawroshe rawshopulawke

(Thammi closes her eyes and listens intently.)

Pawloke pawloke dheu—

CHOTON: Daanra ghumiye porchhe.
[Wait, she's falling asleep.]
O Thammi.
[Hey Thammi.]

(Thammi opens her eyes, irritated. She notices Raheem.)

THAMMI: Ota ke?
[Who's that?]

(Thammi gestures toward the camera.)

CHOTON: Eta Raheem, mone aachhe? Shedin aalaap kawralam?
[This is Raheem, remember? I introduced you the other day?]

(Thammi stares at the camera.)

THAMMI: Shundor dekhte.

(This tickles Choton.)

CHOTON: Tai? *(To the camera)* She says you're "shundor."

(We hear Raheem's voice from behind the camera.)

RAHEEM: What's that?
CHOTON: She thinks you're pretty.

THAMMI *(Inaudibly, her voice catching)*: Handsome.
CHOTON: Ki bolle?
[What'd you say?]
THAMMI *(Feebly)*: Handsome.
CHOTON: Handsome? Hyan handsome.

(He points to the photograph.)

Tomaar bawr-o handsome chhilo. Tai na?
[Your husband was handsome too, wasn't he?]
THAMMI: Hm?
CHOTON: Ei dyakho.
[Look at this.]
Tumi ki tulechhile egulo?
[Did you take these?]

(Thammi looks at the photos for the first time.)

Ei dyakho. Partho.
[Look. It's Partho.]
Chinte parchho?
[Do you recognize him?]

(Thammi stares keenly at the photographs. Something flickers across her face. She looks closer, her eyes searching. She looks as if she's about to say something—
Then she looks away.)

Ke tulechhilo jaano ki?
[Do you know who took them?]

(Thammi notices Raheem again, as if for the first time.)

THAMMI: Ki shundor.
CHOTON: Looks like Thammi's got a little crush on you.
RAHEEM: Tell her I think she's . . . what is it? Shu—
CHOTON: Shundor.

RAHEEM: Shundo. Tell her I think she's shundo too.
CHOTON: Bolchhe tumi-o khub shundor.
[He's saying you're "shundor" too.]

(Thammi's face cracks into a broad smile. Raheem snaps a photo. It develops in the upstage frosted window.)

৭। সেনসিটিভ

7. SENSITIVE

Choton sits at the dining table, on his laptop. The newly developed photos of Dadu are laid out on the table next to him. Raheem is peering into the viewfinder of the camera.

CHOTON *(To himself)*: Or maybe . . . "*still*-colonial"? *(Reading aloud)* "Public Obscenities: Queer Vernaculars in a *Still*-Colonial City"?

RAHEEM *(Engrossed in the camera)*: Huh.

(Choton looks up at him.)

CHOTON: Too much?

RAHEEM: Oh I'm just—don't mind me I'm just tryna figure out where the f-stop is on—

CHOTON *(To his laptop)*: Seriously?

RAHEEM: What?

CHOTON *(Pulling at his face)*: Whyyy are you doing this to me??

RAHEEM: What's—

CHOTON: Can you pass me my charger?

(Raheem walks over to Choton's backpack.)

My battery was 30% like a second ago and now it's literally about to die.

(Raheem plugs the charger into the outlet.)

The . . . switch—

RAHEEM: I know.

(Raheem flicks on the outlet switch. He hands Choton the other end of the charger. Choton plugs it into his laptop.)

CHOTON: I need a new computer.

(Choton types. Raheem peers at him through the Rolleicord viewfinder.)

Ugh, why is everything so *impossible*?

RAHEEM: Have you eaten anything / today?

CHOTON: Like on what planet am I supposed to finish this in the next twenty-four hours?

RAHEEM: You should eat something.

CHOTON *(Typing)*: I had a granola bar.

RAHEEM: . . . you should eat something.

(Choton types. Raheem peers at him through the Rolleicord viewfinder.)

CHOTON: Can I read you what I have?

RAHEEM: Mm-hm.

CHOTON: Or actually—never mind it's— Or whatever, "The title of my project comes from Section 294 of the Indian Penal Code, enacted by the British in 1860. It states," quote, "'Whoever, to the *annoyance* of others, does any obscene act, or utters any obscene song, ballad, or words, in any public place shall be punished with imprisonment.'" Unquote. "The language of this law fascinates me. What constitutes" *(Finger quotes)* "'annoyance'? What was it about the native inhabitants of India that so" *(Finger quotes)* "'annoyed' the British? Were the gender-variant hijras and kothis" *(Finger quotes)* "'obscene,' simply by being? Filming interviews with users of hookup apps like Grindr, Scruff, Planet Romeo, et cetera, this project aims to archive queer and trans vernaculars in—"

(Choton notices Raheem looking down into the viewfinder.)

What are you doing?

(Raheem looks up.)

RAHEEM: I'm listening.
CHOTON: Never mind—
RAHEEM: What? Just—
CHOTON *(Deflated)*: —no, don't worry about it, it's—
RAHEEM: —keep reading.
CHOTON: That's it! That's all I have. This is what I mean, I'm so fucking *slow*.
RAHEEM: Here—
CHOTON: I mean maybe my dad was right, by the time he was my age, Dadu was a college principal, so clearly he knew something about time management that I did not inherit.

(Raheem takes the lid off a dish sitting on the table, revealing kochuri.)

RAHEEM: Just have / like—
CHOTON: I'm / just—
RAHEEM: —*one* of these, they're literally sitting / right here.
CHOTON: —like how is *this* guy . . .

(He indicates the Rolleicord photos.)

. . . *that* guy?

(He points to Dadu's portrait on the wall.)

You know?
Like who is this . . . *man*?

(Raheem peers at the photograph Choton is looking at.)

He just looks so . . .

RAHEEM: Well part of it's like . . . because you're looking down into the viewfinder, you're shooting from below, so it makes him look really tall. Like the photographer clearly made a choice to like . . .

(He looks into the viewfinder, getting lower to the ground, trying to replicate what he's describing.)

—I mean honestly you would have to get pretty low to really—
Wow, yeah, I mean, you basically have to be lying down to get this shot.

CHOTON: I guess I'm realizing . . .
Huh.
That's crazy.

RAHEEM: What?

CHOTON: No I've just . . . I've never seen his smile, right?

(Raheem looks over Choton's shoulder at the photo he's looking at.)

RAHEEM: I mean in this one, whoever took them must've like, cracked a joke or / like—

CHOTON: Like I'm like . . . *(Points to the portrait on the wall) that's* the photo you picked? To represent your dad for the rest of eternity?

RAHEEM: —there's just something about the way the photographer like . . . *captures* him, just like . . . mid-motion . . . like every shot is like, the moment just before he looks, or just after, or like *just* as he's pulling his shirt up, so there's—

CHOTON: Yeah . . .

RAHEEM: —so much life in them.

CHOTON: He just looks so like . . . un-self-conscious, you know? His poite just like . . . casually hangin' . . . just like draped across his chest.

(They stare at the photograph together.)

RAHEEM: I mean these chest hairs—

CHOTON: Right??

RAHEEM: —you would really have to anchor yourself like against a wall or something to get that kind of crisp focus . . .

CHOTON: You think he hired somebody? Like a professional?

(Raheem, anchored against a wall, focuses the camera on Choton.)

RAHEEM: Look at me for a sec.

(Choton looks at him.)

CHOTON: I mean it *had* to have been Thammi, right?

RAHEEM: Right into the lens.

CHOTON: 'Cause who else would he have felt comfortable posing for, like this?

RAHEEM: Like . . . imagine there's a little human in the center of this lens here.

(Choton peers into the lens, brow furrowed.)

OK but relax your forehead, he's just in there, you're not like searching for him.

CHOTON: See this is why I'm not photogenic—

RAHEEM: Or actually . . . close your eyes.

(Choton closes his eyes.)

And when I tell you, open them, and look right at that little person inside the lens.

CHOTON: OK . . .

(Raheem focuses the camera.)

RAHEEM: OK . . . open.

(Choton opens his eyes very wide, deer in headlights. Raheem cracks up.)

CHOTON: *What?*
RAHEEM: Nothing nothing—
CHOTON: You know I suck at—
RAHEEM: No you look great / you're just—
CHOTON: Don't lie—
RAHEEM: Just look at me one more / time.
CHOTON: No.
RAHEEM: Come on, just / one more—
CHOTON: I have to work.

(Choton turns deliberately back to his laptop.)

RAHEEM: Are you actually mad?
CHOTON: I'm just stressed.

(He types.)

And then I need to do a fucking *work* sample, like . . .

(Raheem kisses him on the top of his head.)

RAHEEM: You're doing great.
CHOTON: I'm really not though.

(He pulls at his face.)

I just feel like I don't *have* anything.
RAHEEM: What about all the footage we got yesterday—

CHOTON: Yeah but they weren't like . . . real people.
RAHEEM: The guy at the coffee house?
CHOTON: He did the whole interview in English!
RAHEEM: So?
CHOTON: It was just all kind of like . . . academic. You know? Whereas like Shou . . . like the way they were talking is just so like—like they like, actually identify as kothi and were like, talking about the policeman getting a boner and like—
RAHEEM *(Surprised, intrigued)*: When was *that*?
CHOTON: See you probably didn't even clock it 'cause we were talking in Bangla. They were basically like— Man, I *wish* we'd gotten that on tape. 'Cause *that* would have been an amazing like—like it was just such a *clear* articulation of how . . . queer subjects like . . . see *through* the apparatus of the state to all the like . . . I don't know . . . all the erotic feeling just like . . . simmering underneath and . . . ooo that's actually kind of . . . *(He types)* "all the . . . erotic feeling . . . simmering . . ." *(Trying to remember)* What did I just say? *(Remembering, typing)* ". . . under the . . . apparatus . . ."

(He trails off and keeps typing. Then:)

Can I see it actually?
RAHEEM: What?
CHOTON: Where's your hard drive?
RAHEEM: I mean the footage is still in RAW, I haven't debayered it / yet.
CHOTON: What does that mean?
RAHEEM: You want to look at it right now?
CHOTON: I mean . . . yes I need to make a work sample.
RAHEEM: OK, well, it's gonna take me a second / to—
CHOTON: Can I just look at it myself?
RAHEEM: Do you have Premiere?

(Raheem gets up and walks over to his backpack.)

CHOTON: I mean I'm not tryna—

(Raheem grabs his laptop and sits next to Choton.)

RAHEEM: It's gonna take me a minute to set this up.

(Raheem opens his laptop. Plugs in his hard drive.)

CHOTON: I guess I'm just like . . . how can we . . . I don't know . . . figure out how I can like look at stuff without you having to like, babysit me . . . 'cause I don't want to have to bug you every time I need to look at something . . .

(Raheem finishes setting up the footage in Premiere.)

RAHEEM: Just start at the top?

(Choton looks at Raheem's laptop screen.)

CHOTON: Yeah let's just see what we have . . .

(Raheem starts the footage. Through the laptop, we hear the start of the interview with Shou.)

Yeah we definitely missed the part I'm talking about. When they were like, talking about the cop's "baanra" and like—

RAHEEM: What's "baanra"?

CHOTON: "Baanra" is dick / basically.

RAHEEM: I thought "nunu" was—

CHOTON: I mean "nunu" is more like . . . "wee-wee" right? Wow.

RAHEEM: What?

CHOTON: No just . . . Here I am like thirty years old, and I'm still using baby talk to talk about my body like . . . no wonder I'm such a disaster area.

RAHEEM: What are you talking / about?

CHOTON: I mean maybe I would have been better off *here*. You know? With people that actually look like me like . . . talk like me . . . might actually be *attracted* to me . . .

(Something flickers across Raheem's face. Choton notices.)

What?

RAHEEM *(Bemused)*: I didn't say anything.

CHOTON: I'm just saying I had no language, right? Like I'd never even *seen* another uncircumcised penis. Or talked to / anyone—

RAHEEM: You never saw your dad's?

CHOTON: Are you kidding? Have you *met* my parents?

RAHEEM: I'm just asking.

CHOTON: Have you ever seen them touch?

RAHEEM: Your parents?

CHOTON: I'm just saying—

RAHEEM: I feel like they're pretty affectionate with each / other.

CHOTON: OK.

RAHEEM: Right?

CHOTON: I feel like you're like deliberately playing devil's advocate / or something—

RAHEEM: No I'm just trying to understand 'cause like . . . didn't your parents—

CHOTON: I mean they had a love marriage, sure, but that doesn't—like I don't think *physical* attraction was part of their calculus, right?

(Raheem considers this, brow furrowed.)

I'm just saying there's this skittishness around anything like . . . OK like . . . there was this time in like elementary school, right, when my dad decided we needed swimming lessons 'cause his colleague had drowned in a like freak accident, swimming at the beach . . . Anyway so he would take me to the pool at Stanford and . . . you know, this locker room was full of students and faculty and there were so many penises . . . like I think I even asked if we could go to the women's room 'cause this was still when I would go to the bathroom with my mom when I was with her and . . . Anyway my dad would do this like . . . elaborate choreography . . . like he would wrap his towel around his pants, and then he would take off his pants and his underwear with the towel wrapped around him, and then he would pull his bathing suit on *under* / the towel—

RAHEEM: Yeah I know this trick—

CHOTON: —but then he had this *shirt*, like this like blue spandex shirt he would wear and like . . . here are all these athletes with these like perfect bodies just walking around with their clothes off and *we* were just like . . . covering ourselves up as much as humanly possible. You know?

(He looks at the Rolleicord photos of Dadu.)

Like how is it that no one *ever* said to me—I mean not *once*. Not my dad. Not Pishimoni. Not a single person was ever like— Oh, by the way, your Dadu was— Like I'm not crazy right? I mean look at his *muscles*.

RAHEEM: Yeah . . .

CHOTON: Like what the fuck?

RAHEEM: . . . the way the light is sculpting him really is kind of amazing . . .

CHOTON *(Gesturing to the portrait on the wall)*: Like they basically just turned him into a scarecrow to motivate me to do my homework and like, get into college—

RAHEEM: I mean—

CHOTON: —mm, we only care about him from the neck up anyway, let's just crop out his body and turn him into a like, unsmiling, disembodied head.

RAHEEM: . . . I guess I'm just like . . . like *my* parents, right? Like they had no clue *what* to say to me about college. Or any of it, it was just like . . . a thing they knew nothing about—

CHOTON: Sure . . .

RAHEEM: —and sometimes . . . it kinda sounds to me like you're saying your family's whole focus on education is like a bad thing / and I—

CHOTON: Wait what? When / did I—

RAHEEM: Or maybe not . . . I don't know, I know I don't always have all the like vocab—

CHOTON: —that's not—

RAHEEM: —but I'm like . . . you had a great education, right? Your family loves you. Your family loves *me* which / is—

CHOTON: But . . . how is that what I'm talking about?

RAHEEM: Maybe I don't get what you're talking about.

CHOTON: And maybe I'm not being clear, 'cause like . . . it *is* a super culturally specific thing like . . . like I can *be* gay . . . as long as I get a PhD *in* gay.

(Raheem is deep in thought.)

Does that make sense? Like no wonder I was a virgin till I was twenty-eight, like I never even *pictured* myself having sex. Like even in my own head, I didn't want to be in the fantasy, 'cause having my body in there ruined it—

RAHEEM: But you do now.

CHOTON: Do what?

RAHEEM: *We* have sex.

CHOTON: Yes but—

RAHEEM: You and me.

CHOTON: —but like why can't I pull my foreskin back, right? Why is the head of my penis *so* sensitive that I can't—that *you* can't even touch it—

RAHEEM: But isn't it—

CHOTON: —'cause no one showed me how to pull it back, so it never got stretched out—

RAHEEM: But it's supposed to be sensitive though, right?

CHOTON: Yes but this isn't—like this is about this like cascade effect of like . . . a *long* history of colonial emasculation and / like—

RAHEEM: Can I see?

CHOTON: See what?

RAHEEM: Just—

(Raheem stands Choton up.)

CHOTON: What are you doing?

(The door to the computer room is open.)

RAHEEM: Can I close this door?
CHOTON: Is this the part where you murder me?

(Raheem closes the door. He kneels in front of Choton.)

RAHEEM: Lemme just . . . try, OK?

(He undoes the drawstring of Choton's pajama pant so it falls to his ankles. Raheem takes hold of Choton's penis gently.)

CHOTON: I mean I'm not making this up, I genuinely—
RAHEEM: No I know, but I also don't think you're like . . . broken.

(Raheem gently pulls Choton's foreskin back.)

CHOTON: OK careful, ow—
RAHEEM: Too much?
CHOTON: It's just super sensitive. Like even just the air on / it—

(Raheem blows gently on the exposed head of Choton's penis.)

OK OK—

(He blows a little harder.)

—OK, hold on one—

(Raheem gently inspects the head.)

. . . see those little bumps?
RAHEEM: Mm-hm.
CHOTON: That's—like since my dad *never* talked to me about it, I *never* cleaned the head—
RAHEEM: Have you tried getting hard like this? With it pulled back?
CHOTON: I mean my foreskin is too tight, see that's what I mean.

(Raheem buries his face in Choton's crotch and breathes in deeply.)

RAHEEM: You smell good.
CHOTON: I haven't showered in a couple days.
RAHEEM: Mm-hm . . .
I bet it tastes good too.
CHOTON: . . . I mean . . . it's not that I don't want to, it's just—I mean it's fine with a condom 'cause there's a barrier but like—
RAHEEM: Shh. Just . . . relax. OK?

(Choton takes a deep breath in.)

CHOTON: OK.

(He closes his eyes, as Raheem gently caresses his balls.)

That feels good.
RAHEEM: Yeah?

(Choton breathes out deeply. He opens his eyes. He notices the portrait of his grandfather. It arouses him. Raheem notices.)

Oh yeah?
I thought you couldn't get hard with it pulled back.
You like looking at him?

(Choton squirms, looking at Dadu's portrait.)

CHOTON: He looks so . . . angry . . .
RAHEEM: Yeah?
Did you do something you weren't supposed to?
You been playing with your nunu again?

(Choton looks at Raheem, surprised to hear the Bangla word.)

Yeah? You been a . . . wait how do you say like . . . naughty boy?
CHOTON: . . . dushtu chhele?
RAHEEM *(Trying to pronounce it)*: Dooshtoo chay-lay?

(This makes Choton laugh.)

You been a dooshtoo chay-lay?

(Choton nods, childlike.)

CHOTON: Aamaake shaashon korbena?
RAHEEM: What's that mean?
CHOTON: Aren't you gonna punish me?

(Raheem considers this. Then he closes his hand around Choton's penis. Choton gasps.)

RAHEEM: OK?
CHOTON: Yeah it's just . . . intense.
RAHEEM: Let me know if it's / too much . . .
CHOTON: No no it's . . . I mean I think it feels good, it's just . . . a lot.
RAHEEM: Yeah? You got a sensitive little nunu?

(Choton looks down at this penis.)

CHOTON: It's so little.
So chhoto.
RAHEEM: Doesn't even *deserve* to be called a—what was it?
CHOTON: What?
RAHEEM: The word for / dick?
CHOTON: Baanra?
RAHEEM: Baanra, yeah, doesn't even *deserve* to be called a baanra.

(Raheem takes Choton's penis in his mouth. Choton inhales sharply.)

CHOTON: Fuck.

(Raheem sucks, gently. Choton shuts his eyes.
Jitesh walks in. He sees them. It takes a moment to register what he's seeing. Choton opens his eyes and sees Jitesh standing there.)

Ei—

(Raheem turns to see Jitesh hurrying into the kitchen, avoiding eye contact.)

Fuck.
RAHEEM: Shit.

(Raheem looks at Choton, mortified.)

Fuck.
CHOTON: Ow—

(Choton, with his hand down his pajama pant, is trying to pull his foreskin back up.)

Can you like—help me? I can't get it to—ow.
(Referring to his pajama pant) Can you hold this open?

(Raheem obliges, his attention still focused toward where Jitesh exited.)

See this is why I—it just like, gets stuck.
RAHEEM: Can we like, do this in the bathroom or / something?
CHOTON: It's just painful when it like brushes against the pajama.

(Choton manages.)

I think I—OK OK.

(He reties his pajama pant.)

Wow, there is like *no* fucking privacy in this house.
RAHEEM: Shh!
CHOTON: What?

(Raheem indicates Jitesh in the kitchen.)

RAHEEM: He's like *right* there.
CHOTON: I've told him a million times, if we're working in here, just like . . . knock. You know?
RAHEEM: I feel like we should apologize.

(Raheem is frozen in place.)

CHOTON *(Gently)*: Hey. It's OK.
Seriously.
It's just Jitesh Da.

(He goes to put his hands on Raheem's shoulders, but Raheem avoids it.)

What is happening?
RAHEEM: I'm just—
I think I need a minute.
CHOTON: OK . . .

(Choton sits back down. He waits.)

You OK?

(Raheem doesn't respond.)

Hey . . .
What's up?

(Something moves through Raheem's face. Choton waits. And when he doesn't respond—)

OK fine—

(Choton walks toward the kitchen.)

RAHEEM: What are you—
CHOTON *(Peeking into the kitchen)*: Jitesh Da?
Ay ek second.

(Jitesh enters.)

Tui thik / aachhish toh?
RAHEEM *(To Jitesh)*: Hey I wanted to—

(He realizes he's started talking without knowing what to say.)

Sorry, I—

(Raheem looks to Choton.)

Can you tell him "sorry"?
CHOTON *(To Jitesh)*: Bolchhe sorry . . .

(Jitesh is profoundly embarrassed.)

Kono awshubidha hoyni toh?
JITESH: Na na.
CHOTON: Toke bolechhi na knock korte?
RAHEEM: What'd you say?
CHOTON: He's fine.
RAHEEM *(To Jitesh)*: I'm sorry.

(Choton has an idea. He calls Jitesh over to the table.)

CHOTON: Ei ekta jinish dekhbi? Ei dyakh. Edike ay.

(Jitesh comes over, tentatively. Choton starts playback on the laptop. Jitesh watches himself. He sticks his tongue out and bites it.)

Bhaalo na?
JITESH *(Embarrassed but pleased)*: Hei Raam.
CHOTON *(To Raheem)*: He's probably never seen himself recorded.

(Raheem doesn't respond. They watch the video.)

PISHIMONI *(Offstage)*: Jitesh?

JITESH: Jaii.

(Jitesh hurries off.)

CHOTON: Yeah . . . looks like we got a bunch of him singing but none of that Shou stuff unfortunately . . .

RAHEEM: Well . . .

CHOTON: No I'm not / blaming—

RAHEEM: I said it would take time to set up the shot—

CHOTON: No I know, I'm just—
Like I'm just saying this isn't a "shot" we're "setting up" right? We're just archiving speech acts, so it's more important to just capture the content period / than it is—

RAHEEM: Then why does it matter if I do it?

CHOTON: Whoa.

RAHEEM: You could just set up a camera.

CHOTON: I thought . . . I mean, obviously documenting is a whole skill set—

RAHEEM: But it doesn't really sound like you need a DP.

CHOTON: I thought we—I mean I thought . . . you know, part of this was like . . . we've been wanting to come, and this is a way we could get you here using my grant—

(Raheem is silent. Eventually he gets up. He goes over to his bag and grabs his hat. He returns to the laptop. Saves. Closes his laptop.)

Where are you going?

(Raheem grabs his shoes.)

RAHEEM: Gonna go for a walk.

CHOTON: Wait can we just—
—can we talk about what / just—

RAHEEM: I need a minute. I'm gonna go for a walk.

(Raheem puts on his shoes. He ties his laces. He walks to the gate.)

CHOTON: Hold on, I need to open it.

(He grabs a key from the wall. He unlocks the padlock on the gate. Raheem steps into the stairwell and then remembers something. He walks back into the room. He grabs the Rolleicord from the table. He exits down the stairwell. Choton locks the gate, returns the key to its hook. He sits back down at the table, very still. He stares directly ahead. He pulls out his phone. He stares at it. His jaw muscle twitches. The sound of Grindr messages being sent.)

৮ । প্লেশার

8. PLEASURE

Pishe at his computer, playing billiards with minnesota76.

K_gang	OBSERVE THIS ONE . . .
K_gang	IT WILL STRIKE 6
K_gang	RIGHT SIDE
K_gang	JUST SOFTLY

(Pishe assumes a posture of deep focus. Then he clicks the mouse.)

PISHE: Dhyat!

minnesota76	Oooh almost!
K_gang	WITH COMPUTER ACTUALLY
K_gang	SENSITIVITY IT IS NOT THERE
K_gang	NOT POSSIBLE ACTUALLY
minnesota76	Yeah its not the real thing
minnesota76	Than again I could never play the real thing so this is better for me ;)

K_gang	TRY 10
minnesota76	U think?
K_gang	MAY BE POSSIBLE
K_gang	A LONG THIS SIDE
minnesota76	I'll try . . .
K_gang	GENTLY . . .
K_gang	AHA !
minnesota76	Im surprised that went in!
K_gang	WHAT SURPRISED ?
K_gang	THIS IS STRATEGY :)
minnesota76	Ur pretty good at strategy huh ;)
K_gang	WHOLE LIFE IS A STRATEGY
K_gang	GAME OF STRATEGY
minnesota76	I guess that's right!
K_gang	UR DAUGHTER SHE IS WHAT AGE ?
K_gang	U KNOW YOU DONT LOOK
K_gang	LIKE MOTHER ACTUALLY
K_gang	MOTHER IS HOMELY
K_gang	ISNT IT?
K_gang	IN THE FACE SOME AGING IT SHOULD BE THERE
K_gang	BUT HOW YOU ARE MAINTAINING GIRLISH FIGURE ?
K_gang	PLZ DONT TAKE ANY OFFENCE . . .
K_gang	I MEAN IT IS APPEALING ;)

minnesota76	What do u find appealing . . .
minnesota76	:)
K_gang	U R LOOKING FIT . . .
K_gang	MEANING HEALTHY
K_gang	SHAPELY I MEAN
minnesota76	You look like u have strong arms . . .
K_gang	ONE POINT OF TIME I BOWELED ACUTALLY
K_gang	IN CRICKET CLUB OF DHAKURIA
K_gang	BOWLED !
minnesota76	I would love to see that
minnesota76	I love bowling :)
K_gang	MANY YEARS BACK
K_gang	NOW I AM AGED
minnesota76	I like how you look;)
minnesota76	I think you're very sexy . . .

(Pishe stands furtively and closes the shutters to the computer room. He is invisible to us now. But the conversation continues as projected text.)

K_gang	YOU ALSO ARE
K_gang	SEXY . . .
minnesota76	I wish we were together . . .
minnesota76	In the same place
K_gang	I ALSO WANT THIS
K_gang	PARDON BUT YOU MENTION . . .
K_gang	YOU ARE DIVORCEE OR ?
minnesota76	Im divorced yes

K_gang	U LEFT U R HUSBAND ?
minnesota76	He left actually
K_gang	WHY HUSBAND WOULD LEAVE THAT I DONT KNOW
K_gang	I WOULD NOT LEAVE SUCH A LADY
K_gang	:)
minnesota76	I dont know about that
minnesota76	Dont mind me lets talk about if you
minnesota76	If we were together right now :)
minnesota76	What would we do
minnesota76	;)
minnesota76	Would you let me pleasure you . . .
minnesota76	?
minnesota76	Sorry . . . I didn't mean to make u uncomfortable
minnesota76	Hello ?

(Jitesh enters with a basket of fresh flowers. He can't see Pishe through the shuttered window. He hums to himself, replacing the wilted flowers on the altar. He grabs a hand broom from the corner, reaches up on tiptoes and dusts the top of Dadu's picture frame. The dust tickles his nose. He sneezes.)

৯। ডাইনোসরস

9. DINOSAURS

Jitesh walks over to the table. The photos of Dadu are laid out, just as Choton left them. Jitesh looks at them. He picks one up. He peers at it. The doorbell rings, a tinny ringtone-y "Memory" from Cats. *It startles Jitesh. He walks over to the gate and sees Raheem coming up the stairs.*

RAHEEM: Hey. Sorry, I don't have a key.

> *(Jitesh takes a key from a hook on the wall. He unlocks the gate. Raheem comes in.)*

> Thank you. Sorry—

> *(Raheem notices all the lights are off.)*

JITESH *(A whisper)*: Ghumochchhe shawb.
RAHEEM *(Mimicking his whisper)*: Ah. OK. Sorry.

> *(Raheem unties his shoes. Jitesh hangs the key back on the wall.)*

JITESH: Chaa khaaben?

(Raheem looks up, uncomprehending.)

RAHEEM: Hm?

(Jitesh mimes sipping a cup of tea.)

JITESH: Chaa?
RAHEEM: Oh! No. Thank you. I'm good. Thank you though.

(Raheem clasps his palms in a gesture of thanks. He immediately feels weird about it. Jitesh exits into the kitchen. Raheem collapses back first onto the divan. He stares up at the ceiling fan, fingering the camera around his neck. He pops up suddenly. He goes over to his backpack. He pulls out a little pack of rolling papers. He reaches into his pocket. He pulls out what looks like a bit of crumpled newspaper. Jitesh reenters with a mortar and pestle. He opens Thammi's medicine box. He pops a pill out of its packaging. He glances at Raheem. Raheem notices.)

You want some?

(Jitesh looks at it, uncomprehending. Raheem unfolds the newspaper to reveal some green nuggets.)

Ganja?

(Jitesh smiles in embarrassment.)

JITESH *(Refusing it)*: Na na—
RAHEEM: You sure?

(Raheem puts his finger to his lips.)

I won't tell.

(Jitesh smiles.)

Mind if I—

(Raheem indicates the weed again. Jitesh reads it as another offer. He shakes his head. Raheem takes out a rolling paper. He takes a nugget of weed and begins breaking it apart with his fingers. Jitesh watches. Then he takes two pills and places them in the mortar. He crushes them with the pestle. Raheem watches.)

(Pointing) What's that?

JITESH: Hm?

RAHEEM: That um—

(Raheem thinks. He points again at the mortar and pestle.)

Bangla?

JITESH: Eita?

RAHEEM: Yes.

JITESH: Eita toh haamaandista.

RAHEEM: Itatoha man-dee-sta?

(Jitesh smiles, amused.)

Itatoha man-dee-sta.

(Raheem begins packing his joint.)

JITESH: English?

RAHEEM: Hm? Oh. Yeah it's . . . motor and . . . I actually don't even—

(Jitesh grabs a carton of juice from the fridge. He pours a glass. Raheem meticulously rolls his joint. Jitesh's eyes come to rest on the Rolleicord around Raheem's neck. Raheem notices.)

This?

(Raheem indicates the camera. Jitesh averts his gaze.)

Bangla?

JITESH: Camera?
RAHEEM: But in Bangla?

(Jitesh looks confused.)

JITESH: Hm. Camera.
RAHEEM: Oh it's—ha. I'm dumb. OK.

(Raheem finishes rolling his joint. He pulls out his lighter.)

Sure you don't want some?

(Jitesh shakes his head. Raheem walks over to the window. He takes a hit.)

I like that the windows are just open here.

(Jitesh pours the powdered medicine into the glass of juice and stirs with a spoon. Raheem takes a hit. He notices Jitesh looking at the photos of Dadu.)

They're pretty amazing right?

(Jitesh looks up at him.)

JITESH: Hm?
RAHEEM: The um—

(He considers how to proceed.)

Oh wait—
Chobi?

(Jitesh stares at him.)

Is that—

(Raheem walks over to the table. He holds up one of the photos of Dadu.)

Isn't it . . . chobi?

(They two of them look at the photograph.)

I love the um—

(Raheem touches his own face with his hands, mimicking the photo.)

—hands? I love how crisp they are. With everything else out of focus.
It's beautiful.

(He looks at Jitesh. Jitesh avoids his eyes.)

It's um—
Oh!
No wait.
Shu—
. . . shundo?

(Jitesh looks at him.)

Yes?
This—

(Raheem points at the photo.)

—is shundo?
Shundo chobi?

(Something changes in Jitesh's face. He looks at the photo. For a long moment, they look at the photos together without saying anything. And then: a crow flies in through the window and lands on the table.)

Jesus!

(Raheem jumps out of his seat, knocking over his chair.)

Christ, holy—

JITESH: Oi!

(Jitesh waves his hand in the crow's direction.)

Paala!

(The crow doesn't budge. It cocks its head. Jitesh takes a step closer.)

RAHEEM: Careful.

(Jitesh moves toward the window. He makes a little noise with his mouth. The crow looks at him. Jitesh makes the sound again. The crow preens. Raheem notices the camera on the table. He takes a tentative step forward. He reaches toward it, but just then: the crow caws. Raheem stumbles back.)

Nope. No thank you.

(Jitesh walks to the fridge. He grabs a container of sweets. He opens it. He tiptoes toward the crow.)

JITESH: Oi paagla. Mishti khaabi?

RAHEEM: Careful! It might—

(The bird snaps its beak.)

Bite. Fuck.

(Jitesh walks toward the window with the sweets.)

Wow. Birds really are just dinosaurs.

(Jitesh has an idea. He exits into the internal rooms of the house.)

(To the crow) I see you.

(The bird stretches its wings. Raheem imitates the gesture with his arms.)

Caw!

(The bird looks right at him. Raheem steps boldly forward.)

That's right bitch. I speak your language.

(From offstage, right behind the shut window where Pishe's computer is—)

JITESH: Jaamai Babu?

(Raheem lifts the camera. He points it at the crow. He cocks the shutter. Again, Jitesh from behind the window, more urgently now—)

Jaamai Babu?
(Calling to Pishimoni, a wire of fear in his voice) Didi!

(And just as the crow launches into flight, Raheem snaps a photo.
Blackout. The photo of the crow develops in the upstage frosted window.)

১০। ফিল্ড ওয়ার্ক

10. FIELD WORK

Shou and Choton at the concrete bank of a lake. Raheem's video camera is set up, pointing at Shou.

CHOTON: Aar er shathhe-o ki Grindr-ei aalaap hoychhilo?
[And did you meet him on Grindr too?]

SHOU: Tawkhon kothhay Grindr? Tawkhon Grindr, Romeo kissu chhilo na, didi-ra shawb Lake-ei ghoraphera korto. Ki shundor laagto aamaar shawbaike. Puro moyoor'er moton. Aami shudhu boshe boshe dekhtam.
[What Grindr? Back then there was no Grindr, no Romeo, all the sisters would just cruise by the lake. They were so beautiful to me. Like peacocks. I would just sit and watch.]

CHOTON: Ekhaane?
[Here?]

(Shou points.)

SHOU: Oi je Lake'er maajhkhaane mosjid-ta? Class kete, odike giye boshtam. Ekdin dekhi ekjon purush aamaar dike dyab-dyab kore taakiye aachhe. Tawkhon toh kichhui jaantam na, ekdom-i shishu chhilam. Lok-ta haat tene jigesh korlo, "Kawto?" Aami shaahosh kore bollam, "Amake dekhe maagi mone hoy?" O bollo "Dusho debo." Aami bollam "Teensho." Byas. Jhop jhaar'er moddhye-i shawb khule phello.

[See that mosque in the middle of the lake? I would skip school and go sit over there. One day I saw this guy staring right at me. I didn't know anything back then, I was just a kid. Then he grabbed my hand and said, "How much?" I said, "Do I look like a whore to you?" He said, "I'll give you two hundred." I said, "Three hundred." And that was that. He took everything off, right there in the bushes.]

CHOTON: Taarpawr?

[And then?]

SHOU: Taar aar pawr ki? Khub-i hot chhilo lok-ta, kintu prothhombaar toh? Ki byathha, Ma go Ma, bujhi morlam. Taarpawr thheke aaste aaste gaajor thutu diye aamaar chipti-ta-ke ready korte shuru korlam. Ekhon toh aar kono-i shawmoshya nei. Byanka shoja shawb shawchchhawnde dhuke jay.

[What "then"? The guy was super hot, but it was my first time, right? It was so painful, I thought I was going to die. After that I started getting my "chipti" ready, using a carrot and spit. Now of course I have no problems. Straight, curved, anything slides right in.]

(Shou winks. Choton blushes. He jots something down in his notebook. Shou looks over Choton's shoulder.)

Ki likhchho?

[What are you writing?]

CHOTON: Ei just—

[Just—]

SHOU: Hei Raam.

[Oh lord—]

CHOTON: Ki?

[What?]

SHOU: Chimti na, chimti na go, "chipti."

[Not "chimti," not "chimti," "chipti."]

CHOTON: "Chipti"?

["Chipti"?]

SHOU: Hai kawpaal.

[God help us.]

CHOTON: Aami aashole kawthha-ta shunini aage tai—

[I've actually never heard the word before—]

SHOU: Ki kore shunbe? Eta toh hijra-der bhaasha.

[How would you hear it? This is hijra's language.]

CHOTON: Achchha tumi ki tahle—I actually wanted to ask you—"hijra" kawthha-ta ki—maane tumi ki "hijra" hishebe identify kawro? Kaaron aami toh—

[So do you then—I actually wanted to ask you—does the word "hijra"—I mean do you identify as "hijra"? 'Cause I—]

—a big part of my project is actually looking at . . . ki bolbo . . . the limits, right? Of Anglocentric language like "gay," "straight," / "trans"—

SHOU: Shono everyone they are wanting something special. Tai na? Shudhu gay kothhay, gay, straight, shawbai-i chhoto bela'r thheke aamaar pechhon chutchhe, chhelera chumu khachchhe. Kenoki Shou is a something special. I like this feeling actually. Kintu Ma toh aar sheta bujhbena. Baari'r thheke berolei bolto, why you are putting such gaudy dress, hijra'r moton dekhachchhe, nawjor na tene ektu pawrashona kawr—

[Listen, everyone they are wanting something special. Isn't it? Not just gay, gay, straight, from a very young age everyone was chasing after me, boys were kissing me. Because Shou is something special. I like this feeling actually. Of course my mother can't understand that. Every time I left the house, she would say, why you are putting such gaudy dress, you look like a hijra, instead of calling attention to yourself, focus on your studies.]

CHOTON: Ei je—

[This is—]

SHOU: —aare aami toh chai loke aamaar dike nawjor dik. I want to stand out toh? Stand out na korle, ke pawchhondo korbe tomaake?

[But I want the attention. I want to stand out right? If you don't stand out, who will like you?]

CHOTON: Daanrao ekbaar just—
[Hold on, let me just—]

(He goes over to the camera.)

Aami Raheem-ke exactly *ei* mindset tai bojhano'r cheshta korchhilam—
[I was trying to explain exactly this mindset to Raheem—]

(He notices the "record" light isn't on.)

Wait—
What?
No.

SHOU: Ki holo?
[What happened?]

CHOTON: Wait wait wait—

SHOU: Aare hoychhe-ta ki?
[What's going on?]

CHOTON: Fuck.

SHOU: Ki? Hoyni record?
[What, did it not record?]

CHOTON: I don't think so?

SHOU: Jah.
[Oh no—]

CHOTON: FUCK!

SHOU: Achchha thik aachhe.
[OK, it's OK.*]*

CHOTON: FUCK FUCK FUCK—

SHOU: Aare thik aachhe re / baba.
[OK, come on, it'll be fine.]

CHOTON: Sorry sorry—

SHOU: Ki aar hawbe? Aabaar korbo. Jawkhon khushi, Shou is interview ready.
[So what? We'll do it again. Whenever you want, Shou is interview ready.]

CHOTON: I just have no idea how this fucking thing works.

SHOU: She kothhay? Tomaar director?
[Where is he? Your director?]
CHOTON: We're just . . . I don't know . . .
maane ultimately o toh Bangla bojhena tai . . .
[. . . I mean ultimately, right . . . he doesn't speak Bangla so . . .]
He doesn't always get all the nuances—
SHOU: Hyan ora ektu onnyo rawkom'er hoy tai na?
[Yeah, they're a little bit different aren't they?]
CHOTON: —ei jemon tumi bolchhile tomaar Ma bawle, pawrashona kawr— shaara jibon aami shune eschhi je aamaar Dadu pawrashona-te eto bhaalo chhilo, college'er principal chhilo—
[—like how you were saying your mom says, focus on your studies—my whole life, I've been hearing, my grandfather was such a good student, he was a college principal—]
SHOU: Principal? Ki chaap.
[Principal? That's a lot of pressure.]
CHOTON: Yes! See! But *then* . . . we found these photos of Dadu—oh wait actually—

(He pulls out his phone.)

I took photos of them on my phone.

(He shows Shou his phone.)

Ei dyakho.
[Look.]
SHOU: Eta tomaar Dadu??
[This is your grandfather??]
CHOTON: Right?
SHOU: Dekhi?
[Let me see?]

(Shou takes the phone.)

CHOTON: Jibone keo, ekbaar-o aamaake bawleni je Dadu—
[No one in my whole life ever told me that Dadu—]

SHOU: Sexy laagchhe besh.
[He looks sexy.]
CHOTON: Ei! Ota aamaar Dadu kintu—
[Hey! That's my Dadu you're talking about.]
SHOU: Sheta-i toh bolchhi. Puro zaddy vibes.
[That's what I'm saying. Total zaddy vibes.]
CHOTON: Ha! I mean . . . I guess that is what I / mean—
SHOU: Gonph-ta toh puro Raj Kapoor.
[The mustache is totally Raj Kapoor—]
CHOTON: Doesn't it look like it's drawn on?
SHOU: Oi je. Kaajol'er pencil.
[There. The kaajol pencil.]
CHOTON: Maane?
[What do you mean?]
SHOU *(Pointing)*: Oi je, paashe / ekta—
[There, next to—]
CHOTON: Oh you're right . . .

(Choton peers closer.)

. . . oita ki?
[. . . what is that?]

(Shou removes an eyeliner pencil from their purse.)

SHOU: Ei je.
[Here.]
CHOTON: Ooooh—
SHOU: Laagaabo naki ektu?
[Can I put some on you?]

(Shou moves toward Choton's face with the eyeliner.)

CHOTON: Ki korchho?
[What are you doing?]
SHOU: Aare dekhi na, besh paathaan paathaan dyakhabe. Opor'er dike taakao.
[Oh come on, you'll look like an Afghan warrior. Look up.]

(Choton looks upward. Shou lines Choton's eyes with kaajol.)

Dekhi.
[Let me see.]

(They pull back and look.)

Ba ba—
[Wowee—]
CHOTON: Dekhi—
[Let me see—]
SHOU: Abhi toh party shuru hui hai.
[Now the party's getting started.]

(Choton uses his phone camera as a mirror and looks at himself.)

CHOTON *(Surprised)*: Oh it—
SHOU: Bollam na?
[Didn't I tell you?]
CHOTON: —doesn't look that / bad actually—
SHOU: Raakho eta.
[Keep this.]

(Shou hands him the eyeliner.)

CHOTON: Ki?
[What?]
SHOU: Aare aamaar awnek aachhe, tumi eta / raakho.
[I have so many, you keep this one.]
CHOTON: Aami rekhe ki korbo?
[What am I gonna do with it?]
SHOU: Besh maaniyechhe tomay, phawrsha chehaara toh.
[It looks good on you, you have fair skin.]

(Choton swipes back to the photos of Dadu on his phone.)

CHOTON: I'm just . . .

SHOU: Dekhi chhobi-gulo.
[Let me see the pictures.]

(Shou takes the phone from Choton and swipes through the photos.)

CHOTON: . . . aamaake chirokaal bawla hoychhe Dadu naki ei shawb lok-dyakhano, style maara ekdom-i pawchhondo korto na—
[. . . I was always told Dadu hated all this showing off, posing—]
SHOU: Oh my gawd . . .

(Shou looks mischievously at Choton. Choton notices what they're looking at on the phone.)

CHOTON: Ei ei—
[Hey, hey—]
SHOU: Eta tomaar boyfriend?
[This is your boyfriend??]

(Choton reaches for the phone, but Shou keeps it away from him.)

CHOTON: Ei, please—
SHOU: Aare dekhi na maal-ta.
[Come on, let me see the goods.]
CHOTON: Please dao—
[Please give it to me.]
SHOU: Taar erokom size?
[This is the size of his—?]

(Choton tries to grab the phone.)

CHOTON: Aare!
[Hey!]
SHOU: *Eibaar* bujhlam.
[Now *I get it.]*
CHOTON: Dao na—
[Give it!]

(Choton manages to wrestle the phone from Shou's grasp.)

SHOU: Erom daanda nite byathha laage na?

[Doesn't it hurt to take a rod like this?]

CHOTON *(Coy)*: Aami toh ni na.

[I don't take it.]

SHOU: Mmmm!

(Choton cracks up.)

Ki holo?

[What?]

CHOTON: Na just—aami konodin Banglay erokom aalochona korini / toh—

[No it's just—I've never talked about things like this in Bangla before—]

SHOU: Achchha tomaar baari'r lokjon ki tahle byapaar-ta mene niyechhe?

[So has your family accepted the situation?]

CHOTON: Kon byapaar-ta?

[What situation?]

SHOU: Ei je . . . tomaar je boyfriend—

[You know, that you have a boyfriend.]

CHOTON: Hyan shedik diye khub-i progressive, Raheem ke shawbai bhaalobaashe—

[Yeah, from that point of view, they're very progressive, everyone loves Raheem—]

SHOU: Tomaader deshe toh shunechhi aajkaal biye-o kawra jay—

[In your country, I've heard you can even get married these days—]

CHOTON: Aamaar desh maane?

[What do you mean my country?]

SHOU: Americay naki gay marriage—

[Don't you have gay marriage in America?]

CHOTON: Eita-i toh aamaar desh.

[This is my country.]

SHOU: Korbe na biye?

[You're not gonna get married?]

CHOTON: Ke?

[Who?]

SHOU: Aha kawro na, aami ashbo.

[Oh come on, do it, I want to come.]

CHOTON: Tumi aashbe? Tahle toh korte-i hawbe.

[Well if you're *coming, I have to.]*

SHOU: Hyan kawro kawro. I *love* biyebari.

[Yes, do it, do it, I love *weddings.]*

CHOTON: Aaj shawkaale aamaar Thammi-ke ei chhobi-gulo dyakhachchhilam. Bollam, ei dyakho tomaar bawr. Thammi dekhe bollo: "aamaar ekhono biye-i hoyni."

[This morning I was showing my Thammi these pictures of Dadu. I said look it's your husband. Thammi said, "I'm not even married yet."]

SHOU: Aha re ki sweet. Aamaar khub-i sweet laage buro maanush-der ei kawthha-gulo shunte. Shesh awbosthhay aamaar Thakurda ekebaare bachcha-der moton hoye giyechhilo.

[Isn't it sweet? I love when old people start talking like that. At the end, my grandfather was like a little baby.]

CHOTON: Thammi'r o *exactly* tai. Aaj dekhe mone hochchhilo . . . *aamaar* buro boyoshe . . . dhawro aami deathbed-e . . . aar Raheem-i roychhe shaathhe, aamaake comfort kawra'r cheshta korchhe . . . bole jachchhe, it's OK, it's OK, kintu aami bujhte paarchhi . . . maane more jachchhi je . . . aar aami bolchhi, "Bhoy korchhe. Aamaar bhishon bhoy korchhe" . . . kintu o toh bujhte paarchhena . . . kaaron aami Banglay bolchhi . . . aar aami bujhte paarchhi je o bujhte paarchhena . . . aar or-o bhoy korchhe kaaron . . .

[Thammi is exactly the same. I was looking at her today and thinking . . . like in my old age . . . like imagine I'm on my deathbed, right? And Raheem is the only one there, and he's trying to comfort me . . . He keeps saying, it's OK, it's OK, but I can tell . . . I mean . . . that I'm dying . . . and I'm saying to him . . . "I'm scared. I'm so scared" . . . but he doesn't under-

stand me, 'cause I'm speaking in Bangla . . . and I can tell that he doesn't understand me . . . and he's scared too 'cause . . .] He can see . . . that I'm dying . . . and he doesn't know what I'm saying.

SHOU: Esho.
[Come.]

(Shou taps their lap.)

Ekhaane esho.
[Come here.]

(Choton, recognizing the familiar maternal gesture, lays his head in Shou's lap. Shou gently massages Choton's head.)

Ma ke bollam. Hollywood thheke eschhe. Aumurto Da.
[I told Ma. This guy's here from Hollywood. Aumurto Da.]

(Choton smiles to himself.)

Ki holo?
[What?]

CHOTON: Na just—aamaake toh keo Aumurto bole daake na / tai—
[No it's just—no one calls me "Aumurto," so—]

SHOU: Maane?
[What do you mean?]

CHOTON: Bhaalo naam dhore toh keo-i daake na.
[No one calls me by my good name.]

SHOU: Ki bole daake tahle?
[What do they call you then?]

CHOTON: Choton bole-i daake.
[They call me Choton.]

SHOU: Choton?
[Choton?]

CHOTON: Aare oi deshe toh keo jaanena je aamaake "Choton" bole berachchhe, oder kaachhe toh ota-i aamaar naam.
[I mean in America they don't know that they're calling me "little one," to them that's just my name.]

(From the nearby mosque, through loudspeakers, the call to prayer.)

SHOU: Shundor laage na? Aamaar aajaan shunte khub romantic laage.
[Isn't it beautiful? I find listening to the call to prayer so romantic.]

(They listen.)

CHOTON: Aamaader kaachhei Islamic Center of North Hollywood aachhe ekta, tai prottek din-i azan shuni. Kintu ekhaane shunechhi bole mone pawre na.
[There's an Islamic Center of North Hollywood right near us, so I hear the call to prayer every day. But I don't think I've ever heard it here.]

(The call to prayer sounds again. Shou plays with Choton's hair.)

SHOU: Tomaake dekhe mote-i Choton mone hoy na.
[You don't look like a "Choton."]
CHOTON: Dadu-i diyechhilo naam-ta.
[Dadu gave me that name.]
SHOU: Dekhi aar ekbaar, chhobi-gulo?
[Let me see the pictures?]

(Choton hands Shou his phone.)

Shotti-i ki handu chhilen tomaar Dadu. Hubohu tomaar moton dekhte.
[Your Dadu really was so handsome. He looks just like you.]
CHOTON: Ki bolchho?
[What?]
SHOU: *Hm.* Puro twins.
[You're twins.]
CHOTON: Dhyat.
[Nonsense.]

SHOU: *Shotti.* Mukh bawshano puro.
*[*Really. *You have the same exact face.]*

(Choton looks up at Shou. Shou notices him looking. Sebanti, an elder hijra, heavily made-up, in a colorful sari, enters the theater. She sees them gazing at each other. Choton reaches up and touches Shou's face.)

SEBANTI: Olebaabaaa. Eke aabaar kothhar thheke peli?
[Oh myyyyy, where'd you find this one?]

(Choton startles. He sits up.)

SHOU: Oi je bollam na, bidesh thheke eschhe, Aumurto Da—
[Remember I told you? This is Aumurto Da, from America—]

SEBANTI: Mmm! Ki shundor laagchhe dujonke. Agal bagal. Ekdam bar-bahu.
[Mmm! You two look so cute together. Side by side, bride and groom.]

(Shou rests their head on Choton's shoulder. Choton blushes.)

Ba ba, ki lawjja!
[Look at you blush!]

SHOU: Sebanti Di aamaader shawbai-ke bhaalobaashe. Aador kawre, jawtno kawre.
[Sebanti di loves us. She dotes on us, takes care of us—]

(Choton puts his palms together and says, to Sebanti:)

CHOTON: Nomoshkaar.
[Greetings.]

SEBANTI: O baba. Namaste Babuji.
[Oh my. Greetings, good sir.]

(Sebanti sits and massages her feet.)

SHOU: Jaano Aumurto Da Hollywood-e thhaake?
[You know Aumurto Da lives in Hollywood?]

CHOTON: Aare North Hollywood ekta neighborhood'er naam, "Hollywood"er shaathhe kono-i shawmporkho nei, puropuri immigrant elaaka—
[No no, North Hollywood is just the name of a neighborhood, it has nothing to do with "Hollywood," it's a totally immigrant area—]

SHOU: Achchha o deshe tomaar ki visa go?
[What visa do you have over there?]

(Choton is surprised by the question.)

CHOTON: Aamaar? Toh . . . US citizenship.
[Me? I . . . have US citizenship.]

(Shou clucks their tongue.)

SHOU: Ki kawpaal go tomaar. Aamaar kawtodin dhore ichchha America jaowa'r.
[You're so lucky. I've wanted to go to America for so long.]

(Sebanti notices an audience member staring at her.)

SEBANTI: Ki dekhchhen Didi?
[What are you looking at sister?]

(Shou follows Sebanti's gaze.)

Dekhun, bhaalo kore dekhun.
[Look. Take a good look.]

SHOU: Jolchhe puro hingshay.
[She's burning with jealousy.]

SEBANTI *(To Choton)*: Dekhish. Haate baajare gele-i bhawdromohila-ra phish phish kore bawle: "eto shundor blouse kothhar thheke baaniyechho, tomaader moto bawro gawla'r blouse porte aamaader khub bhal-laage, kintu jaano-i toh aamaader shaami aachhe, bachcha-kachcha aachhe, oder shaamne toh pawra jay na." Jaara pawre toh aamaader dekhe-i pawre. Emonki cinema'r heroine-ra-i toh aamaader shundorjo dekhe copy kawre.

[When I go to the market, all the ladies whisper to me: "Where did you get such a beautiful blouse made? We love wearing the kind of low-cut blouses you wear, but you know, we have husbands, we have kids, we can't dress like this in front of them." Those who do wear them are modeling themselves after us. Right? Even movie actresses try to copy our beauty.]

SHOU: Aumurto Da kintu bikkhaato director.

[You know Aumurto Da is a famous director.]

CHOTON: Aare—

SEBANTI: Tai naki?

[Is that so?]

CHOTON: —bhul dhorechho byapaar-ta—

[You're getting this all wrong.]

SEBANTI: Nibi shona aamaake?

[Will you take me sweetie?]

SHOU: Aare orokom noy, eta documentary cinema—

[It's not that kind of film, this is a documentary—]

CHOTON *(To Sebanti)*: Shunun aapni ki aamaar shaathhe ekta interview korte chaiben?

[Listen would you be interested in doing an interview with me?]

SEBANTI: Interview maane?

[Interview meaning?]

CHOTON *(To Sebanti)*: Aami aashole ekta research project niye eshechhi—

[I'm actually here on a research project—]

SHOU: Achchha ei kaaj-ta'r jonnyo visa paowa jaabe na?

[So couldn't I get a visa for this work then?]

CHOTON: Tar maane?

[What do you mean?]

SHOU: Aami toh aashole tomaar moton-i korte chai. Cinema, acting egulo-i—

['Cause I actually want to do what you do, cinema, acting—]

CHOTON: Daanrao—

[Hold on—]

SHOU: This is my dream actually. Creative / work—

SEBANTI *(To Shou)*: Jaanish serial-e aamaake ekbaar nite cheyechhilo? Director aamaake *khub* pawchhondo korechhilo.
[You know I almost got cast in a TV series? The director really took a liking to me.]

(Shou cracks up at this.)

CHOTON: Eta kintu cinema noy, eta ekta—
[This isn't a movie, it's a—]

SHOU: Jani aami—
[I know—]

CHOTON: —ekdom-i onnyo / byapaar—
[—it's a totally different thing—]

SHOU: Aare byapaar-ta bujhechhi, aamra documentary subject. Tai toh?
[I know, I get it, we're documentary subjects. Right?]

CHOTON: Orokom documentary-o na / thik—
[It's not even a documentary like—]

SHOU: It will show India-te, kirokom gay, transgender-der otyachaar—
[It will show, in India, how gay, transgender folks suffer—]

CHOTON: Na na—
[No no—]

SHOU: Thik dhorechhi kina?
[Did I get it right?]

CHOTON: —ekdom-i na—
[—not at all—]

SHOU: Tahle?
[Then?]

CHOTON: —it's not that kind of—it's not about "showing" anyone anything—
—eta maane . . . aami toh aamaar nijer—aamaader queer community'r jonnyo-i / toh toiri korchhi.
[I mean this is . . . I'm looking at my own—I'm making this for our queer community right?]

SEBANTI: Thaak baba, aami awto kichhu bujhina, queer-feer / aami—
[Listen I don't know much about all this "queer" business, I'm—]

CHOTON: "Queer" / bolte—

["Queer" meaning—]

SEBANTI: —shaadhaaron maanush, aashirbaad korlam.

[—a simple person. Here's my blessing.]

(She touches the top of Choton's head. Choton reaches down to touch her feet.)

Ei ei, aamaar pa chhuite nei, Bramhon maanush. Aamaake pronaam kawre na babu, aamaake chhalla dyay.

[Hey hey, you don't touch my feet! You're a Brahmin. You don't pay respects to me dear, you give me "chhalla."]

(She claps resonantly and extends her hands to Choton.)

CHOTON: "Chhalla" maane?

[What's "chhalla"?]

SEBANTI: Shono. Tumi cinema kore rojgaar kawro. Sebanti Di'r rojgaar toh eta-i. Eta-ke bhikkha bawle na, aamaader bhaashay eta-ke chhalla bawle. Mouli Mata-ka chhalla.

[Listen. You earn by making movies, right? Sebanti Di earns like this. We don't call this begging. In our language, we call this "chhalla." "Chhalla" for Goddess Mouli.]

(Choton jots in his notebook.)

CHOTON *(Confirming)*: "Mouli" Mata?

[Goddess "Mouli"?]

SEBANTI: Proshno'r kintu awbhaab nei.

[He's got a lot of questions doesn't he?]

CHOTON: Sorry sorry—

(He pulls out his wallet.)

Aami toh aashole aapnaader bhaasha niye khub interested, kaaron aamaar nije'r kaaj-ta . . .

[I'm actually very interested in your language 'cause my own work is—]

(He takes stock of what's in his wallet.)

Oh shit.
Aamaar kaachhe shudhu dollar-i aachhe dekhchhi.
[I actually only have dollars.]

(He pulls out a twenty-dollar bill.)

SEBANTI *(Impressed and amused)*: Ba ba—
[Oh wow—]
SHOU: Dekhi?
[Let me see?]

(Shou intercepts the bill before Sebanti can take it.)

SEBANTI: Ei!
[Hey!]
SHOU: Eta kawto taaka hawbe?
[How much is this in rupees?]
CHOTON: Kuri dollar toh . . . praay du haajar / hawbe?
[Twenty dollars is . . . almost two thousand?]
SHOU: Du haajar??
[Two thousand??]
SEBANTI: Ei chor! De.
[Hey thief! Give it.]

(Sebanti tries to grab the money, but Shou plays a game of keep-away.)

Shuonrer bachcha!
[Son of a pig!]

(Sebanti grabs the bill from Shou, who is enjoying themself thoroughly.)

Shaaheb jaamai jutiyechhish bhaaloi.
[You found yourself a good foreigner husband huh?]

(She stuffs the bill into her blouse.)

(To Choton, in her best American accent) Thank you very much.

(This cracks Shou up.)

(To Choton) Bhaalo thhaakish baba, shusthho thhaakish.
[Take care dear, be healthy, be well.]

(She exits singing a Bollywood song, an inside joke. Shou cackles.)

CHOTON: Aami ki bhul korlam kichhu?
[Did I say something wrong?]

(Choton's phone rings. He picks up. Shou tries to get ahold of their giggles.)

(Into the phone, curtly) Hey.
I'm just—

(His face darkens with concern.)

What?
Are you—
I'm coming.
No, I'm coming right now.
I'm on my way.

A SHORT FILM

INT. A HOTEL ROOM—DAY

A thin shaft of light peeks through a gap in the window curtains. The room is empty. A desk. A bed. A mirror on the wall. Then the door opens with a click. Light floods in from the hallway, and in walks a man, wearing all white, a tan leather portfolio in hand. The door swings shut behind him. He steps forward into the shaft of light, and we see that it is PISHE. His eyes glance around the room, taking stock of where he is. He notices himself in the mirror: the white outfit, the portfolio. He's seen this somewhere before, but he can't quite remember where. He walks to the window. As he pulls back the curtain, CUT TO:

PISHE's perspective, looking through the window, out onto a swimming pool. The pool seems empty, but then a woman breaks the surface, wipes the water from her eyes. The camera zooms in to reveal it is PISHIMONI, shaking her hair, water droplets flying off her in *Baywatch* slow motion. She catches PISHE's eye, watching her through the window. CUT TO:

PISHE closes the curtain and turns back into the hotel room to see: a WOMAN in an elegant bottle-green sari, sitting at the edge of the bed, staring at the wall. She turns to look at him. It is PISHIMONI. Extreme close-up of her eyes, full of longing, lined with kaajol like a Bollywood heroine. The camera zooms in.

DISSOLVE INTO:

EXT. A RIVERBANK—DAY

Close-up of PISHIMONI's bare feet, walking right along the edge a river. The river starts to rise and her feet are underwater. CUT TO:

A close-up of PISHIMONI, her hair in two schoolgirl braids. Water splashes on the camera, her hands up in the air, silently mouthing, "Baanchao, baanchao." Subtitles read: "Save me, save me." And as she falls back, CUT TO:

EXT. A GREEN FIELD—DAY

PISHE, in his white suit, catches PISHIMONI in his arms as she falls. She is in her bottle-green sari again. She looks up at him with gratitude à la *Gone with the Wind*. A crescendo of Bollywood strings. "Mera Sapnon Ki Rani" starts to play. They lip-synch to it, dancing through the field, playing peekaboo. Then abruptly, the sound of a crow. PISHE turns, and CUT TO:

Black and white. PISHE in a dhuti, a basket on his head. Absentmindedly, he catches something invisible in the air and puts it in his basket. Catching. Putting. Catching. He walks away from us, out of focus, and disappears into the distance.

১১। বিকামিং এ পিকচার

11. BECOMING A PICTURE

Raheem and Choton in the sitting room, each paging through a photo album.

RAHEEM: What about this one?

(He points to a photo in the album he has. Choton looks.)

CHOTON: I mean . . . it's not great . . .
RAHEEM: Yeah . . .
CHOTON: I just want one that actually looks like him. You know? He would have *hated* this.
RAHEEM: We'll find one.
CHOTON: I mean the whole thing, all of this, putting people up on an altar.

(Choton shakes his head.)

So stupid.

(He walks over to the bookshelf to grab another album.)

Like have you seen either of them leave the house even one time, this whole week we've been here? Jitesh is literally the only person that leaves this house. Everyone else is just lying around and eating sweets all day like—

(He considers whether to ask the following question. Then he asks it anyway.)

Why didn't you call me right away?

RAHEEM: What do you mean?

CHOTON: Like when you found / him.

RAHEEM: I did call.

CHOTON: No I know / but—

RAHEEM: I called as / soon as—

CHOTON: —I was only two minutes away, I could have been here by / the time—

RAHEEM: I mean Jitesh was trying to get him out of the chair all by himself, I had to like, help carry him down the stairs and into the taxi 'cause Pishimoni / like—

CHOTON: Like what fucking century are we in? People are dying because we can't call an ambulance? Like—

RAHEEM: I mean I know this isn't—but like . . . I mean I think he'd been there for a while . . .

CHOTON: And nobody noticed?

RAHEEM: . . . I mean the shutters were closed, I couldn't—

CHOTON: No I know I'm just . . . trying to understand . . .

RAHEEM: I mean I had just gotten back. And when Jitesh found him . . . and then Pishimoni was trying to like, wake him up, but like . . .

(He trails off, reliving the situation.)

CHOTON: Where did you go? When you left.

RAHEEM: I just . . . walked. I ended up at the—is it the Academy of Fine Arts?

CHOTON: You *walked* to Rabindra Sadan?

RAHEEM: It wasn't that far. Then I went over to the Victoria Memorial. This guy saw me taking pictures and was like, hey you want some ganja? And I was like, what, you see a Black man and you just assume I want drugs?

CHOTON: But you got some.

RAHEEM: I mean . . . I definitely got some.

(Choton arrives at the end of the photo album he's looking through.)

CHOTON: Why is it so hard to find one good picture of Pishe?

(Choton grabs another album. He brings it over to the dining table.)

RAHEEM: Sorry I walked out like that.
I just needed some space.
I don't know. It's been a lot honestly.

(Choton thumbs through the album.)

CHOTON: I just felt kind of abandoned.
Like we were having this like—I mean I *thought* we were having this like, intimate moment and then you just—

RAHEEM: I know.

CHOTON: —and when you leave like that, I just—like I have no idea what you're thinking and my brain just starts to—I don't know. Kinda makes me go a little crazy.
And I know that's something I need to—I know I need to learn to self-soothe or whatever, but like—I mean it's hard when I'm constantly having to—I mean I *love* being here with you, but it's—it's exhausting constantly having to translate between like—I mean I wanna make sure *you're* OK, and make sure Pishe and Pishimoni are / like—

RAHEEM: I get that.

CHOTON: And I know that's not on you but—I don't know.
I don't know.
I mean my uncle just died. I should've been here. You know? Not doing a stupid interview.

(Choton lets out a sad little laugh.)

I didn't even get it.

RAHEEM: What?

CHOTON: I mean I forgot to press record.

RAHEEM: . . . shit . . .

CHOTON: Yeah.

RAHEEM: . . . sorry . . .

CHOTON: Why are *you* sorry, I'm the dumbass who thought I could just like, do it myself like, "I'll show you!"
I don't know . . . it was weird. Felt weird. There was a moment . . . I don't know . . .
. . . I feel like maybe they were just using me? Like I was this American they could just—
Anyway. I guess it doesn't matter now.

RAHEEM: You could probably get an extension though, right?

CHOTON: I don't know . . .

RAHEEM: Just email them and be like, my uncle just died, I need an extra day.

CHOTON: . . . yeah . . . I think I feel kind of relieved honestly. 'Cause when shit like this happens, you get to be like . . . yeah, no, I'm not doing the "application," sorry I was actually . . . lighting a body on fire . . .
It all feels so . . .

(Choton looks over to Pishe's computer.)

. . . like every time I come, he just wants me to play pool with him, right? Or not even play, I think he just wanted to like, show me. Like I think he just wanted me to watch him.

(Raheem puts his hand on Choton's shoulder.)

So stupid.

RAHEEM: Hey . . .

CHOTON: Like how does a city with twenty million people have like no emergency medical services?

RAHEEM: Yeah . . .
CHOTON: You know? Like it's actually like, criminal.

(For a moment, the two of them are lost in their own thoughts.)

RAHEEM: You know he told me about this dream he had?
CHOTON: What? When?
RAHEEM: Was that yesterday?
CHOTON: What did he say?
RAHEEM: I don't know, he had this dream. And it was crazy, 'cause in the dream he was watching a movie, in a movie theater. And he basically like . . . described the whole movie to me.
And then he told me to go make it . . .
CHOTON: What do you mean?
RAHEEM: Like he was like . . . you're a director. Go make this movie.
CHOTON *(Amused)*: What?
RAHEEM: And I was like—
CHOTON: What was the movie?
RAHEEM: It was this like . . .
I don't know . . .
It's kind of hard to describe . . .

(Raheem pictures it. A man in a white suit. A woman in a green sari.)

CHOTON: Maybe we should make it.
RAHEEM: I don't know . . .
I guess I've been thinking . . .
CHOTON: About?
RAHEEM: No just about like . . .
I don't know . . .
Like . . . I used to think I didn't *want* to make my own work, you know?
But I don't know, being here . . . I feel like maybe that was a little bit of a cop-out?
CHOTON: But you do / make—
RAHEEM: Just let me—

CHOTON: Sorry—

RAHEEM: —like OK sometimes . . . like I'll just wake up with a song stuck in my head . . . but it's not a song that exists, it's a song that was just like there in my dream . . . but then when I try to remember it, like if I try to record myself singing it or anything it's just like . . . gone. But *he* like . . . I mean he remembered this whole movie. You know? Like shot for shot.

. . .

CHOTON: I mean there *is* this grant I was looking at. Through FWB. For collaborations between scholars and practitioners.

RAHEEM: Yeah . . .

CHOTON: I don't know, it could be kind of . . . Dream as Archive . . .

RAHEEM: Yeah . . . that's not really what I'm thinking about right now—

CHOTON: For sure, I just meant / like—

RAHEEM: Like I think I need to figure out what *I* want to make. You know?

(Pishimoni enters with a tray of neem leaves.)

PISHIMONI: Tora snaan korishni?

[You haven't showered yet?]

CHOTON: Ei geyser-ta chaalalam—

[I just turned on the hot water—]

PISHIMONI: She ki ekkhuni ja, shawshaan thheke phire-i snaan korte hoy.

[What? Go right now, you have to shower when you get back from the crematorium.]

CHOTON: Jachchhi. Pishe'r chhobi-ta dekhe nichchhilam—

[I'm going, I was just figuring out Pishe's picture—]

PISHIMONI: Ei ne.

[Here.]

(She hands him a neem leaf.)

CHOTON: Ki eta?

[What's this?]

PISHIMONI: Neem paata.

[A neem leaf.]

CHOTON: Pishimoni . . . aar koyekdin-i roychhi, er moddhye pet khaaraap / hole—

[Pishimoni, we're only here for a few more days, if we get a stomach bug—]

PISHIMONI: Aare toder mineral water diye-i dhuyechhi. Ne. Cheba bhaalo kore.

[I washed it with your mineral water, don't worry. Here. Chew it.]

(Choton puts the neem leaf in his mouth, uncertainly.)

Rohim?

RAHEEM: What's this?

PISHIMONI: This is neem leaf, for purification.

CHOTON: Baba re ki teto.

[It's so bitter.]

(Raheem puts the leaf in his mouth. Pishimoni notices the album.)

PISHIMONI: Peyechhish chhobi?

[You found a picture?]

CHOTON: Eta bhaalo na, onnyo ekta khunjchhi.

[This one isn't good, I'm still looking.]

PISHIMONI: Dekhi?

[Let me see?]

CHOTON: Eta ekdom-i bhaalo na.

[This one's bad.]

(For a long moment, Pishimoni looks at the photo of Pishe.)

PISHIMONI: Shawbai chhobi hoye gelo . . .

[Everyone's a picture now . . .]

(She closes her eyes. She inhales deeply. She begins to recite, quietly, in Sanskrit.)

debi proponnartihare praseeda

(Choton puts his arms around her.)

praseeda matarjagatohikheelasya
praseeda bisheshwari pahibishwang
twameshwari debi charaacharasya

(Raheem's eyes are wet. After a long moment, Pishimoni's eyes open.)

Tora snaan korte ja. Jitesh toh ekhono death certificate-er pechhon chhute berachchhe.
[You two go and shower. Jitesh is still running around trying to get the death certificate.]

(Pishimoni exits into Pishe's computer room.
Choton notices Raheem is crying.)

CHOTON: Hey . . .
Hey hey . . .
Come here—
RAHEEM: Sorry—
CHOTON: Come.

(Choton pats his lap. Raheem curls up into it.)

RAHEEM: I don't know why I'm crying—
CHOTON: It's OK . . .

(Choton caresses Raheem gently, giving him "shushshuri.")

It's OK . . .
PISHIMONI *(Offstage)*: Eta toh na.
[Not this one.]
CHOTON: Ki korchho?
[What are you doing?]

PISHIMONI *(Offstage)*: Pisher Aadhar Card-ta khunjchhi.
[Looking for Pishe's Aadhar Card.]
CHOTON: "Aadhar Card" maane?
[What's an "Aadhar Card"?]
PISHIMONI *(Offstage)*: Ei re. "Aadhar Card" ki kore bojhabo jaanina.
[I have no idea how to explain an "Aadhar Card."]

(Pishimoni exits to the inner rooms.)

RAHEEM: Thanks for the shushshuri.

(Choton smiles down at him.)

CHOTON: Anytime.

(For a moment, they are still, and quiet, together. Just the gentle rhythm of Choton's shushshuri.)

RAHEEM: I can't believe I'm in India . . .
CHOTON: I am so ready to go home . . .
You know what I miss? I miss Mexican food . . .
I miss our bed—
RAHEEM: Oh you know what?

(Raheem lifts his head up, remembering something.)

CHOTON: What?
RAHEEM: I took a picture of him yesterday.

(Raheem walks over and grabs the Rolleicord from the table.)

CHOTON: Really?
RAHEEM: Yeah when he was telling me the dream.
CHOTON: With the Rolleicord?
RAHEEM: We could probably get the film back in a day or / two—
CHOTON: I mean that could be kind of perfect.
PISHIMONI *(Offstage)*: Ei Rohim!

RAHEEM: Yup?

PISHIMONI *(Offstage)*: Come. You can reach this—

CHOTON: Ki?

RAHEEM *(Exiting)*: I / got it.

PISHIMONI *(Offstage)*: Tui ja snaan korte!
[You go shower!]

(Choton takes off his clothes, soiled from the crematorium, and wraps his towel around his waist. He notices himself in the mirror. His own reflection looks different to him. He adjusts his posture. Gently, he traces the contours of his chest with his fingertips. Then he exits into the bathroom.)

১২। ফ্যামিলি ফোটো

12. FAMILY PHOTO

Pishimoni, Choton, and Raheem in the sitting room. Packed suitcases, camera gear, backpacks. A large photo of Pishe has been set up on the altar, a bulky flower garland hung around the frame. It's the photo Raheem took: Pishe, looking piercingly at the camera, smoke curling out of his mouth.

CHOTON: You grab your phone charger?
RAHEEM: Yup.
CHOTON: Passport?

(Raheem pats his pocket.)

PISHIMONI: Aar ektu kichhu kheye ja.
[Have something to eat before you go.]
CHOTON: Na beshi khele aabaar awshshosthhi laagbe.
[No, if I eat too much I'll feel nauseous.]
PISHIMONI: Kichhu pack kore di tahle.
[Then let me pack you something.]

CHOTON: Aare dawrkaar nei, awnek granola bar aachhe.
[It's OK, we have lots of granola bars.]

PISHIMONI: Rohim?

RAHEEM: Hm?

CHOTON: You hungry?

RAHEEM: Oh no I'm good thank you.

PISHIMONI: Dekhi gaari-ta eshe pounchholo kina.
[Let me see if the car has come.]

(Pishimoni looks out the window.)

CHOTON: You got all your gear and everything?

RAHEEM: Pretty sure.

PISHIMONI: Dekhchhina toh.
[I don't see it.]
Dhyat. Mobile-ta aabaar kothhay raakhlam?
[Where did I put my mobile?]

CHOTON: Ei je.
[Here.]

(Choton sees Pishimoni's phone on the divan. He hands it to her.)

PISHIMONI: Kawtobaar kore lok-ta-ke bollam—
[I told that man so many times—]

(Pishimoni dials.)

Hello, Mr. Mitra? Gaari kothhay? Baarota'r shawmoy aashar kawthha chhilo na?
[Hello, Mr. Mitra? Where is the car? It was supposed to arrive at noon.]

(She listens.)

"On the way" maane? Aamaar bhaipo eschhe America'r thheke, return flight paanchta'r shawmoy—
[What do you mean "on the way"? My nephew has come from America, return flight is at five o'clock—]

(She listens.)

Bollei holo? International flight-er reporting tin ghawnta aage.
[Excuse me? International flights must report three hours beforehand.]
Hm.
[Yes.]
Achchha gaari-ta—
[And the car—]
(To Choton) ei Dadamoni kawtay eshe pounchhochchhe re?
[Hey what time is Dadamoni arriving?]

CHOTON: Dekhchhi daanrao.
[Let me see.]

(He searches on his phone.)

PISHIMONI *(Into the phone)*: Gaari-ta kintu bhor-raat porjonto laagbe, mone aachhe toh?
[You remember we need the car overnight, right?]
Hm.
[Yes.]
Next du shawptaaho laagbe puro, Mr. Ganguly has expired.
[We need it for a full two weeks, Mr. Ganguly has expired.]

(She listens.)

Dekhun aapnaar ki mone aachhe, ki mone nei, ta aami ki jaani?
[Look I don't know what you do and don't remember.]
Hm.
[Sure.]

CHOTON: Yeah, he's arriving at—

PISHIMONI *(Into the phone)*: Thik aachhe. Raakhlam.
[OK. OK bye.]

(She hangs up.)

CHOTON: 2:20 A.M. Emirates-er flight.

PISHIMONI: Tahle airport-e neme gaari-ta aabaar paathiye dish. Raatre aabaar Dadamoni-ke tulte paathiye debo.

[Then when you get to the airport, send the car back. I'll send it back tonight to pick up Dadamoni.]

CHOTON: I wish we could stay.

PISHIMONI: Tui toh aashol shawmoy-ta-tei chhili.

[You were here for the real part.]

CHOTON: I know, but still. Kaaj'er jonnyo thhaakle toh bhaalo hoto.

[It would have been nice to be here for the service.]

PISHIMONI: Tor toh phire giye awnek kaaj.

[You have lots of work to get back to.]

(Choton sighs.)

CHOTON: Ki je kaaj.

[Yeah . . . work . . .]

PISHIMONI: Kaaj thhaaka toh bhaalo babu.

[Having work is a good thing.]

(Pishimoni looks at the photo of Pishe. Her gaze lingers on him.)

Besh hero-hero laagchhe na?

[Doesn't he look like a movie hero?]

(To Raheem) He would have liked this photo, you know?

(A car honks outside.)

RAHEEM: I actually—

PISHIMONI: Oi je gaari eshe gechhe.

[There, the car's here.]

RAHEEM: —wanted to say thank you.

PISHIMONI: Hyan?

[What?]

RAHEEM: I just wanted to thank you. For—

PISHIMONI: O baba, aabaar "thank you"? Kisher "thank you" babu?

[Oh goodness, "thank you"? Thank you for what babu?]

RAHEEM: No really, you did so much, feeding us, taking care of us. And for letting me use the camera.

(Pishimoni points to the Rolleicord, which is around Raheem's neck.)

PISHIMONI: Take it with you.
RAHEEM: No, no, I think it should stay here.

(Raheem places the camera on the dining table.)

PISHIMONI: Here it is only gathering dust.
RAHEEM: I'll just have to come back and use it then.
PISHIMONI: Yes please come again. This is your home.
(To Choton) Khub pawchhondo hoychhe aamaar. Simple chhele, kono shawmoshya nei.
[I have really taken a liking to him. Simple boy, no trouble at all.]

(Choton chuckles.)

Homely ja-ke bole.
[What we call "homely."]
CHOTON: Who you calling homely?
PISHIMONI: Yes, homely.

(She reaches up and holds Raheem's face affectionately.)

Ekdom baari'r chhele'r moton.
[Just like a member of our home.]
CHOTON: Oh shit did you grab the toothpaste—
RAHEEM: Yeah, I got it.
PISHIMONI: Itinerary ki re toder, ekhaan thheke?
[What's your itinerary from here?]
CHOTON: Kolkata to Delhi. Delhi to Newark. Newark to Los Angeles.
PISHIMONI: Baba re. Aamaar ekhaan thheke Delhi jete-i ja awbosthha—
[Goodness. I can barely manage flying from here to Delhi.]
CHOTON: Last time I came the in-flight video was broken on the way back. Sixteen hours—
PISHIMONI: *Sixteen?*

CHOTON: —zero movies.

PISHIMONI: Ei chaanachur-ta bhule jaash na kintu.

[Hey don't forget to take the chaanachur!]

(Pishimoni hands Choton an enormous packet of bhujia.)

CHOTON: Pishimoni—kothhay dhokabo eta?

[Pishimoni—where am I gonna put this?]

RAHEEM: Here, I have space in my backpack.

CHOTON: You sure?

(Raheem takes it from Choton.)

PISHIMONI: Aabaar aashbi kawbe?

[When will you come again?]

CHOTON: Aashbo shiggiri.

[I'll come soon.]

(Pishimoni reaches up and holds Choton's face.)

Tumi kawbe aashbe bawlo?

[When are you coming?]

PISHIMONI: Kothhay?

[Where?]

CHOTON: America?

[America?]

PISHIMONI: Thhaak baba.

[No thank you.]

CHOTON: Keno?

[Why?]

PISHIMONI: Ei aamaar shaathhe ekta chhobi tulbi na, jaowar aage?

[Hey aren't you going to take a photo with me before you go?]

CHOTON *(To Raheem)*: Hey can you take a picture of us?

RAHEEM: Sure.

(Pishimoni squeezes Choton's face.)

PISHIMONI: Shona chhele aamaar.
[My sweet boy.]
He is like my son, you know?

(Raheem picks up the Rolleicord.)

CHOTON: Oh you're gonna take it with that?
RAHEEM: Don't worry I'm gonna take one with my phone / too.
CHOTON: No, do it, I like that. There's film in there?
RAHEEM: Here, let's do it this way—

(Raheem turns so that his back is to the light.)

PISHIMONI: Ei Rohim, come in the photo. Ei Jitesh!
RAHEEM: I got it—
CHOTON: He *wants* to take it, Pishimoni.

(Jitesh enters.)

PISHIMONI: Ei aamaader ekta chhobi tule dite paarbi?
[Can you take a picture of us?]

(Jitesh looks uncertainly at Raheem. Raheem offers Jitesh the Rolleicord. Jitesh takes it. Pishimoni beckons to Raheem.)

Come. Family photo.

(Raheem squeezes between Pishimoni and Choton. Pishimoni puts her arm around Raheem. Jitesh hangs the camera around his neck. He opens the viewfinder. He looks down into it. He adjusts the camera settings, like someone who knows them intimately. He takes his time. Focus. Aperture. Shutter speed. The others hold their pose, smiling stiffly. Jitesh cocks the shutter. Winds the film—)

O jaane? Ki bhaabe—
[Does he know? How to—]

(The camera clicks. Blackout. For a split second, the still contour of Jitesh and the camera glows in the darkness. A cacophony of crow calls.)

END OF PLAY

Shayok Misha Chowdhury is an Obie and Whiting Award–winning writer and director. *Public Obscenities*, his playwriting debut, was one of three finalists for the 2024 Pulitzer Prize for Drama. Misha's many-tentacled practice in theater, music, poetry, and film has earned him The Relentless Award, the Mark O'Donnell Prize, a United States Artists Fellowship, a Princess Grace Award, a Jonathan Larson Grant, two Sundance fellowships, and a Fulbright Fellowship.